'What a delight ... it reflections and d... ... its pages a fascinating mix of characters – some familiar and others not so much – whose stories bring to life the Way of Love to which Jesus calls us all. These reflections and the accompanying questions will both inform and inspire you in your own ongoing journey.'
The Most Revd Michael B. Curry, Presiding Bishop of The Episcopal Church

'Full of storytelling, memoir and theological reflection … Easy to read but packed with depth and insight, [*Stick with Love*] takes us on a journey in the inspirational company of the saints of God, from many parts of the world and periods of history. This is a wonderful Advent companion in the journey towards Christmas.'
Dr Paula R. Gooder, Canon Chancellor of St Paul's Cathedral, author and speaker

'In a world where difference can be exploited for hate, injustice, violence and oppression, this book models how to stick with love. Using stories of people from throughout the world, Bishop Arun Arora beautifully embodies the new community that Jesus both offers and energises – a new community of justice, grace and hope. A must-read book for Advent for both individuals and groups.'
The Revd Professor David Wilkinson, Durham University

'Bishop Arun leads us through Advent with his characteristic wisdom and insight. This is an exciting way of engaging with one of the most spiritually intense periods of the Church's year ... a wonderful book.'
Canon Giles Fraser, Vicar of St Anne's. Kew, journalist and broadcaster

'Reading this was like spending an afternoon with Bishop Arun at the pub, where he warmly introduced me to some fascinating people who all had something unique to teach me about faith. *Stick with Love* encourages us to pull out the tent pegs of the Church and stretch the canvas to cover more people and invite them into the story of God. It is brimming with Advent hope.'
The Revd Jayne Manfredi, BBC Radio 4 'Thought for the Day' contributor and broadcaster

'A beautifully written Advent book, which brings its stories in an accessible but challenging way, carried by giants of faith, some of whom you'll know and some of whom you might be meeting for the first time ... Bishop Arun gathers the beautifully diverse family of faith around the table to learn and reflect as we prepare for the great feast that is to come.'
Canon Kate Bottley, priest, journalist and presenter

Arun Arora is Bishop of Kirkstall in the Anglican diocese of Leeds, and was formerly a minister in the Church in the North-East, West Midlands and North Yorkshire. He has served as Director of Communications for the Archbishop of York and subsequently for the National Church Institutions of the Church of England. Arun has written widely for national and regional papers, including *The Guardian*, *The Times*, *The Independent*, the *Yorkshire Post*, the *Birmingham Post* and the *Northern Echo*, where he was a columnist. In 2021, he co-chaired the Archbishops' Anti-Racism Taskforce which produced the report *From Lament to Action*.

To my mother, Sudarshan, who said yes at Villa Park.
To my wife, Jo, who said yes when I asked.
To my daughter, Indie, God's yes to our prayers.

Stick
with
Love

**Rejoicing in every tongue,
every tribe, every nation**

Arun Arora

First published in Great Britain in 2023

SPCK
SPCK Group
Studio 101
The Record Hall
16–16A Baldwin's Gardens
London EC1N 7RJ
www.spck.org.uk

British Library Cataloguing-in-Publication Data
A catalogue record for this book is available from the British Library

ISBN 978–0–281–08985–7
eBook ISBN 978–0–281–08986–4

3 5 7 9 10 8 6 4 2

Typeset by Fakenham Prepress Solutions
First printed in Great Britain by Clays Ltd

eBook by Fakenham Prepress Solutions

Produced on paper from sustainable sources

Contents

Foreword by the Archbishop of York   ix
Introduction   xii

THE FIRST WEEK OF ADVENT

The First Sunday of Advent: St Francis Xavier   1
Monday 4: St John of Damascus   6
Tuesday 5: Isaiah 56:1–8: salvation for others   10
Wednesday 6: St Nicholas, Bishop of Myra   14
Thursday 7: St Ambrose of Milan   19
Friday 8: Revelation 7.9–12: before the throne of God 24
Saturday 9: Helen Berhane   29

THE SECOND WEEK OF ADVENT

The Second Sunday of Advent: Leah Sharibu   35
Monday 11: Asia Bibi   40
Tuesday 12: The Revd Canon Jemima Prasadam   46
Wednesday 13: St Lucy of Syracuse   51
Thursday 14: St John of the Cross   56
Friday 15: George Floyd   60
Saturday 16: Dr John Sentamu   65

Contents

THE THIRD WEEK OF ADVENT

The Third Sunday of Advent: Cardinal Francis-Xavier
   Nguyen Van Thuan   70
Monday 18: Eglantyne Jebb   75
Tuesday 19: The Rt Revd Francis Loyo   80
Wednesday 20: Stormzy   85
Thursday 21: Charlie Freer Andrews   90
Friday 22: The Revd Billy Graham   95
Saturday 23: The Revd Dr Florence Li Tim-Oi   100
Christmas Eve: The Revd Dr Martin Luther King:
   stick with love   105

Notes   110

Foreword

The times and seasons of the church calendar often lead us to a consideration of where we find our meaning and purpose as disciples of Jesus Christ. This richly rewarding Advent book provides three different ways of entering into that process.

The first is story. Jesus was a master storyteller and taught his followers in parables, some of which end with questions. So, in the parable of the two sons, we're asked, 'Which of the two did their father's will?' In the parable of the houses built on rock and sand, the question is, 'Which house will survive the storm?' And, famously, after telling the parable of the good Samaritan, Jesus enquires of his interlocutor, 'Who was the man's neighbour?'

In the daily stories of the saints who appear in *Stick with Love* (some widely recognised, others less well known), we encounter women and men whose lives are resonant with the love of God. Their music is part of our own story and song: with joy and lament they enable us to encounter afresh the surprising, all-surpassing love of God. Whether in saints from ages past or saints still living, the grace of God at work is a reminder of the importance of grace in our own lives – and of how fundamental that undeserved love is to our own self-understanding. Not all of us could respond so robustly to some of the trials we learn about here. But these stories of trust, hope and love are a demonstration of the power of faith in the midst of trial.

The second way we find meaning is through our relationships. We read of women and men from across the globe, representing every tribe, tongue and nation. These are people who are part of the family of the Church that stretches through time and encompasses us too.

Reflecting on some of the chapters that draw on Arun's own story, it is hard but necessary to acknowledge that there are times when our family links and common, shared identity – which is to be found in baptism and in the Eucharist – are affected by attitudes and actions that sadly speak more expressively of difference and otherness.

That we are part of a global Church, a worldwide family, should always be a matter for rejoicing. In the meantime, whether our family is to be found in lands where Christians are persecuted for their faith, or in countries where faith is openly flourishing, our call to rejoice with those who rejoice and to mourn with those who mourn is a reminder of our mutual belonging. The Apostle Paul's use of our physical body as an image for the Church in 1 Corinthians is a reminder that where one suffers, the whole will be in pain; where another part is honoured, all may rejoice.

Advent is the season of the Christian year when we anticipate not only the birth of Christ, but also what the Church calls the 'last things'. The Bible speaks of this in the book of Revelation, particularly the vision of every tribe, people and nation gathered together before God and finding salvation in Jesus. It is a vision of diversity and unity, mirroring the very life of God.

And so, the third way of entering into the process of finding our meaning and purpose as disciples is, of course, through Christ himself. Jesus is the common thread to be found in each of the lives of those featured here – from St Lucy to Leah Sharibu and St Nicholas to Stormzy. We read of people touched through encounter with Jesus and explicitly shaped and formed in response to him.

Stick with Love issues a real challenge to us to go deeper in our journey of discipleship. May you discover this Advent a renewed appetite for the transforming love of God, and a fuller understanding of what it is to be a disciple committed to responding to that love.

Stephen Cottrell
Archbishop of York

Introduction

There are various traditions we associate with Advent, whether it be the evergreen wreaths to be found hanging on front doors; the Advent candles lit each week in churches; or the calendars now available in endless variations of daily offerings, from chocolate to pork scratchings to lip balm (all three of these have made an appearance in my household over the years). One of the newer traditions is the now annual debate on parts of social media as to whether Advent should be marked as a season of expectation, celebration and hope, or whether it should be more penitential in tone – a time for meditating on the last things of death, judgement, hell and heaven. To accompany our Advent journey this year, I have tried (in the best Anglican tradition) to navigate a middle way through these approaches, offering stories and reflections that are full of hope, alongside questions that may pose real challenge.

This book is rooted in two biblical images with a common theme.

The first is to be found in Isaiah 56, where we read about those who will be brought to God's holy mountain where the Temple will be a house of prayer for all nations, a description referenced by Jesus in Mark's Gospel. The second image is found in Revelation 7, where we encounter a vast multitude – from every nation, tribe, people and language – standing before the throne of God. These images remind us of the universal nature of the Church, a global body of women and men spanning the centuries, from every conceivable context and corner, united in their common belief. From those two images have emerged stories of individuals from across the world, from antiquity to the present age, whose lives speak of a divine love and the triumph of hope. Of course, not every nation is represented in these pages; alongside those from the UK are people from India, Italy, Vietnam, Uganda, Nigeria, Eritrea, China, Pakistan and the USA, to name but a few.

Some of the women and men included, such as St Ambrose of Milan, St Nicholas of Myra, St Lucy of Syracuse and Eglantyne Jebb, are commemorated by the Church of England in its liturgical calendar for the month of December. Others who feature are Christians whose stories also provide reasons for hope and, importantly, for reflection, particularly when they include experiences of suffering and imprisonment. We are reminded that, even today, there are places in our world where to declare a faith and hope in the Christ who will come again can lead to kidnap, torture, imprisonment and death. As we undertake our own spiritual MOT during Advent, and spend time examining our hearts, these stories serve to remind us of all who need our prayers, as they undergo the kind of tests and trials that have faced the saints down the ages.

Inevitably, those selected to appear in the book are my personal choice. I've been inspired by many of the Church's saints, and alongside them are other everyday saints I have had had the privilege of encountering or knowing, who have shaped, formed and helped me. Finally, I have included people I have never met but who have been heroes of the faith for me. One of those is the Revd Dr Martin Luther King, whose 1967 speech 'Where Do We Go from Here?' provided the title *Stick with Love*, and supplies the basis for the final reflection on 24 December.

I owe grateful thanks to Stephen Cottrell, who graciously asked me to write this volume for Advent 2023. His joy in a Church of all tribes and nations inspired the book, as did his ongoing commitment to racial justice. My particular heartfelt thanks (and constant apologies) go to Alison Barr, Publisher at SPCK, who was charged with the task of overseeing the writing process and whose empathy and goodwill I pushed to the limit. Any errors that remain in the text are mine alone.

It has been said that, statistically speaking, the average Anglican is female and African. The fact that the stories in this book do not reflect that picture points to how much more I have to learn about the untold stories that sit alongside those that appear here. I would like to dedicate *Stick with Love* to the women who have shaped and go on shaping me on my own journey, and to whom my debt of gratitude continues.

Arun Arora
Leeds

The First Sunday of Advent
St Francis Xavier

But Christianity is not an English religion, Mum. There were Christians in India a long time before there were Christians in England. There are more Christians in India than there are in England, more Christians than even Sikhs. Christianity is not a white religion, Mum.

I was 16 years old when I took the decision to be baptised as a Christian. I had been attending my local Baptist church in Birmingham for some months, having made a commitment to follow Jesus a few years earlier. The day of my baptism was approaching and I had invited my mother to come and be part of the congregation that day.

It would be fair to say my mother wasn't a fan of the decision I was about to make. A few months earlier, a friend who had just been released from a young offenders' institution (or Borstal as it was then known) was looking to do something on a Friday night that carried less risk than his previous activities. His mum and sisters attended a local Baptist church which ran a youth club on Friday nights. My friend and I went along and, after a few weeks, the man who organised it asked what I was doing on Sunday morning. 'Nothing,' I replied. He asked whether I would be interested in coming along to church. I went and kept going.

One of my mother's objections to my decision was that I was selling out. I came from an Indian family; my mother was Hindu and my father Sikh, so why did I want to become a Christian, my mother asked? She thought I was being brainwashed by the culture around me, giving up my identity and who I really was.

I was aware of her concerns and was happy to set the record straight.

My answer, such as those given above, cut little ice.

Part of my mother's objection lay in her experience and understanding of how Christianity had spread in northern India, which was shaped by the practice of some of the missionaries of making what were known as 'Rice Christians'. These were Indians who converted to Christianity, sometimes even taking an English name as a sign of their conversion, in exchange for material benefits, such as a bowl of rice. Theirs wasn't so much a conversion of the heart and mind as the answering of a practical need born of grinding poverty and hunger. Those willing to exploit such circumstances for religious advantage didn't come highly rated.

With such a view of the propagation of the gospel, it was entirely understandable that my mother cried in church on the day of my baptism. Hers were not tears of joy. As I confessed with my lips and believed in my heart that Christ was Lord, my mum's objections remained. At home we had a roof over our heads and food on the table. We had our own rice. Why become a Christian?

Many years later, I found myself in Goa accompanying a group of Further Education students on a trip to southern

India, the cradle of Indian Christianity and the resting place of St Francis Xavier (1506–52). Francis is buried in the magnificent Basilica of Bom Jesus, having been responsible in his short lifetime, it was claimed, for the conversion of more than half a million people, mostly in India.

There is no suggestion that Francis used the tactics of some of the missionaries who would follow him in converting people to Christ. However, the uneasy relationship between Western empires and missionary endeavour was evident during the four-century colonisation of parts of southern India by the Portuguese, which began in 1505 and lasted, astonishingly, until 1961. The strictures of the Western Church imposed on the local church in the sixteenth century would lead to schism and suppression in the decades that followed Francis's death.

Francis was not the first Christian to evangelise India. That honour is reputed to have been given to St Thomas the Apostle, the doubting disciple, who is credited with founding a number of churches and communities in southern India fourteen hundred years before Francis arrived. If the churches of Corinth, Ephesus and Philippi held the Apostle Paul as their founding father, so the churches of Kodungallur, Gokamangalam and Niranam were believed to have viewed Thomas in the same way. The subsequent growth of the Church, linked with the arrival of Persians and Syrians, meant that by the time of the Council of Nicaea in AD 325, one of the delegates recorded as present was John, Bishop of Persia and India. The churches began to be known as the Mar Thoma Church – the Aramaic for St Thomas.

According to some ecclesiastical accounts, by 1599 with the arrival of the Portuguese, the Mar Thoma Christians were being asked to recant their faith and practice in order to embrace the Latin version of Roman Catholicism. This was formally achieved at the Synod at Diamper, leading to the destruction of historical records, liturgies and prayer books of the Mar Thoma Church that were declared heretical by the Synod. Fifty years later, those who regarded themselves as St Thomas Christians sought to rebel against what had been decided at the Synod, with thousands of laity and clergy marching to Coonan Fort to declare independence from Rome and the Portuguese. This assertion – known as the Oath of the Bent Cross – has been described by Mar Thoma churches as 'a declaration of independence against foreign aggression over the sovereign right of the Christians of India'.[1]

Today, Mar Thoma churches are found across the world, mirroring the Indian diaspora, in places as diverse as North America, Europe, Singapore, South Africa, Australia, London, Liverpool and Solihull.

Ultimately the complexities of empire, colonialism and mission, whether British or Portuguese, cannot fully obscure the truth of the gospel and the love of Christ. It's a truth that breaks free from whatever chains of oppression are placed upon it. But as Thomas and Francis Xavier demonstrate, the authenticity of the gospel is always to be found simply in the sacrificial service it inspires.

Questions for reflection

1 Thomas the Apostle is most often referred to as 'Doubting Thomas' due to the Gospel accounts of his witness of the resurrected Christ. Does his missionary activity in India lead you to reconsider his legacy and how one moment can define a reputation?

2 The mixing of colonialism, empire and missionary work was evident in India both with the Portuguese and the British. How can we recover a sense of the message outshining the method?

3 Financial control, either through reward or deprivation, is a tactic that some churches employ in disputes with other parts of the church. Can such actions ever be justified?

Monday 4
St John of Damascus

In celebration of Black History Month back in 2004, the newspaper *New Nation* published the results of a poll conducted to determine the greatest black icon of all time. The competition was fierce, with Martin Luther King, Malcolm X, Muhammad Ali and Nelson Mandela all making it into the top ten of the 100-strong list, alongside perhaps less obvious contenders such as Oprah Winfrey, then the highest-earning black woman in history. Alongside her was Mary Seacole, the pioneering nurse who earlier that year had been voted the greatest black Briton in a BBC poll.

Yet despite the enormous achievements of each of these men and women, none of them managed to make it to the top spot. The winner of the vote for the greatest black icon of all time was, in fact, Jesus Christ.

Surprised? Admittedly, to some people the thought of Jesus as a black man is rather shocking, especially if the images of Christ they are familiar with are those to be found in the art of churches across the UK.

I trained for the priesthood in the North-East, which included spending time at Ushaw College in Durham, one of four Roman Catholic seminaries in England operating at the time. The main chapel at Ushaw is stunning, a place of marvellous beauty, serenity and spirituality. Yet, a glimpse of its glorious stained-glass windows reveals numerous images of Jesus with hair so golden it would put any self-regarding platinum blonde to shame.

The blue-eyed, blonde-haired Jesus puts in another appearance at Cranmer Hall, Durham in the college chapel of St Mary the Less. The crucified figure above the altar looks more like a man from Jesmond than Jerusalem.

There will be those who say that, by depicting God in our own image, we serve to bring Jesus closer to the people and it is only natural that we should follow the renaissance depictions of a 'whitewashed' Jesus.

But what if the image of a black Jesus had been more commonplace in our history? Try to imagine for a moment the impact on the slave traders of Liverpool, Cardiff and Bristol if they turned up at church each Sunday to worship a Christ whose image bore a striking resemblance to the chattel they had purchased the previous day.

Images of Christ, reflecting the very physicality of his incarnation, have the power to inform not only how we understand God, but also how we treat one another. Seeing the divine spark in the face of a fellow human being is more possible if it resonates with our own image of Jesus.

Today, the Church of England marks St John of Damascus, the eighth-century monk, who is one of the fathers of the Eastern Orthodox Church and perhaps best known, at least in the West, for his strong defence of the use of icons as part of worship.

In AD 726, Emperor Leo III ordered the destruction of all icons throughout the Byzantine Empire. This campaign for the physical smashing of images – 'iconoclasm' – was rooted in a theological understanding that the Old

Testament forbade graven images and the worship of them. Advocates of iconoclasm equated the veneration of icons with idolatry, arguing that such practices replaced the worship of the divine.

A fundamental part of the argument John of Damascus put forward in defence of icons was that the Incarnation – God taking flesh and entering into human history as Jesus Christ – changed everything. John wrote three treatises against 'those who attack the holy images', in which he differentiated between the veneration of icons and idolatry. While icons enabled worship through adoration, they were not the true object of worship, he argued. Worship was not offered to icons themselves but to what they represented, and such veneration did not amount to idolatry, as it did not offer worship to something other than God.

After Leo's death in 741, the new Empress Irene called the Second Council of Nicaea in AD 787. This restored images to all the churches and removed the ban. Although the issue resurfaced in the following century, with a further ban, the matter was finally resolved in 843 when the Empress Theodora allowed their restoration.

More than a millennium later, the focus on images has never been more prevalent, especially among the young. The advent of digital technology and mobile communication has driven the use of social media and especially image-dominated media. Platforms such as Instagram and TikTok are designed for visual imagery, as is YouTube. Between them, these three platforms alone accounted for 5.5 billion monthly users in January 2023.

Yet, despite the dominance of image-based media, there is little to be found in the digital space when it comes to icons. Reverential images of Christ in a newly imagined form fit for a digital era remain relatively rare. One of the reasons for this might be related to the iconoclast's unease. In a digital space, where images are notoriously debased and where pornography is widespread, might there be a wariness about the place of holy images?

Yet if John of Damascus was right and the Incarnation does indeed change everything, then there is nowhere in heaven or on earth – in the digital space or in the physical world – where Christ's reign does not extend. For a new generation, who live so much of their lives in an everyday digital gallery of images, how will they encounter the image of Christ? And through it see that image in the faces and lives of others?

Questions for reflection

1 The use of icons remains prevalent in the Orthodox and other Churches. Why do you think they are so much less employed in the West?
2 What impact do you think a more widespread use of the imagery of a 'black Jesus' would have had on Britain's empire and the slave trade?
3 Do you share the unease of the iconoclasts when it comes to the use of images of Christ in the digital space?

Tuesday 5

Isaiah 56:1–8: salvation for others

'Where are you from?'

It's a question that I have been asked many times in church – occasionally when I've been on holiday and visiting as a worshipper in a new place; more regularly when I've been a visiting preacher in the Church of England or on various circuits of the Methodist Church.

My usual answer is simply 'Birmingham'. As the place where I was born, brought up and spent the first three decades of my life, Birmingham is most definitely where I am from. On more than a few occasions, however, this answer has seemed insufficient to those enquirers. 'Yes, but where are you really from?' they ask.

'I really am from Birmingham,' I reply. Sometimes I lay this on a bit thick, following it up with a phrase in pure Brummie, its wonderfully warm accented cadences leaving any interlocutor in no doubt of my West Midlands homeboy credentials.

Sometimes this will be enough, and those with ears to hear will recognise that I have doubled down on their original question and am not keen to go to where their enquiry might be heading – to focus on my foreignness. We smile, move on to other topics of conversation, perhaps whether they have been to Birmingham, have ever had to experience its notoriously difficult inner ring road, or have family connections to that divine city. At other times, though, the questions keep coming.

'But where are you originally from?'

Ah. Often, at this point, I confess, my mood can dictate how I respond. I know that many who persist do so without an iota of ill intent. They are trying to be friendly, perhaps nudging the conversation around to the fact they have once been to Asia, they've had history with family or friends who look like me, and they're seeking in some way to build a bridge based on my appearance, on the colour of my skin. Sometimes a convoluted conversation about the weather has ensued – a noting of how cold it is, and how I must be unused to such weather where I come from. (My reply has been to assure them that the weather in Birmingham is often subtropical.)

While often innocent and well meaning, these questions can lead to an underscoring of difference; a reminder that I am 'foreign', as much as my birth, passport and upbringing suggest otherwise. Although we may have shared a common cup minutes earlier, emphasising our common baptism and identity in Christ, the end of the service sometimes somehow gives way to a reintroduction of otherness and the things that set us apart rather than those we share together.

On one occasion, having presided and preached at a service, filling in for a holidaying clergyman, I was asked by a member of the congregation not only where I was from but what religion I was. While this may have been a fairly damning comment on the quality of my sermon, it left me wondering how far the questioner was able to see past the colour of my skin to the possibility that I too was a brother in Christ. Had the words of my mouth in the offering of the eucharistic prayer and proclamation of the good news of Jesus Christ all been drowned out by the non-verbal communication present in my brown skin?

Isaiah 56 is often considered to be the start of Third Isaiah (or Trito-Isaiah) with its focus on the post-exile people of God who have returned to Jerusalem. (Many of the themes arising in the earlier part of Isaiah, such as repentance, justice and hope, recur in chapters 56 – 66.)

The opening verses of the chapter focus on two groups who have traditionally found themselves excluded from belonging to the people of God – eunuchs and foreigners. Isaiah's word from the Lord offers not only hope to these groups but a vision of full belonging and blessing.

Both groups are invited to keep the Sabbath and hold fast to the covenant, alongside God's chosen people. For the eunuchs, the promise is 'a memorial and a name better than sons and daughters; I will give them an everlasting name that will endure for ever' (v. 5). To the foreigners the promise, set out at verse 7, is an invitation to be brought to God's holy mountain and given joy in 'a house of prayer for all nations'.

While this message provides hope to the excluded, it's unclear whether the people of God were ready to accept those who were treated as outsiders by virtue of birth or ritual uncleanliness. Was their 'otherness' readily overlooked by those who belonged as they returned to Jerusalem trusting in the promises of God?

One thing that is unambiguous is that the salvation brought by Jesus Christ was open and offered to *everyone*.

We see this most clearly in Philip's encounter with the Ethiopian eunuch in Acts 8, where Philip is instructed to go to the desert road from Jerusalem to Gaza. There he meets a man in a chariot reading the Scriptures – a passage from Isaiah 53.

Beginning with that passage, Philip explains to the high-ranking Ethiopian official the good news of Jesus who fulfilled Isaiah's prophecy. As his eyes are opened to Christ, he asks Philip to baptise him. Philip leads the eunuch down into the water where he is baptised into the faith. We are told that he went on his way rejoicing – it really didn't matter where he was from.

Through that encounter, one more person found their way into God's house of all nations, where God's invitation was accepted and the worldly divisions of global borders were dissipated in the waters of baptism. A new belonging was found in a common faith and the prophecy of Isaiah we read about today attained emblematic fulfilment.

Questions for reflection

1 What barriers do you observe for those who would seek to make a home in our churches who may have been born abroad or come from a different cultural background?

2 Are there people who wear a modern mantle of 'eunuchs', who may feel they would not be welcomed in a house of prayer or might consider themselves to be excluded?

3 If you happened upon someone asking you to explain the Bible and the good news of Christ to them, how would you do it? Where would you begin? What might you say?

Wednesday 6
St Nicholas, Bishop of Myra

If I asked you to close your eyes for a moment and picture St Nicholas, I wonder what kind of picture would come to mind?

Would it be that of a fourth-century saint of Turkish origin who was made Bishop of Myra while still a young man and became known for his generosity to those in need, for rescuing sailors in the Aegean Sea, for his love for children and his concern for the destitute?

Or would it be the image seen in the Netherlands, Belgium, Luxembourg and northern France, of a white-bearded bishop dressed in red cope and mitre, who on 6 December is celebrated with the festival of Sinterklaas?

Or would you think of a portly, jolly, white-bearded man, with a red hat and sometimes with spectacles? This last image we owe to the American cartoonist Thomas Nast, whose original drawings were of a small Santa (he later became full size) who could slide down chimneys. Nast was the first to draw Santa wearing a red suit with fur lining, a nightcap, and a black belt with a large buckle. This image has been maintained and reinforced through song, radio and advertising, not least by Coca-Cola who used Nast's red-suited Santa in their adverts from the 1920s onwards.

The conversion of Nicholas from saint to Santa has brought with it a change in our expectations. The question posed by every modern-day Santa to the children they meet in our shopping centres at this time of year is: 'Have you been a good boy or girl?' An affirmative response leads to the production of a present. I don't know what happens if the answer is more nuanced.

But it was an altogether different question that led to St Nicholas being remembered in church history. That question was, who is Jesus?

In AD 325, Emperor Constantine convened the Council of Nicaea, the very first ecumenical council. More than 300 bishops came from all over the Christian world to debate the nature of the Holy Trinity. The fruit of their labours is reflected in the Nicene Creed which we still recite in churches today.

Some of the delegates led by Arius, an Egyptian bishop, insisted that Jesus was not fully God in human flesh. They agreed that Jesus was sent in a very special way from God. They even agreed that Jesus is the 'son of God' in the sense that God was so pleased with Jesus' performance that he made him his son by adoption. But they insisted that Jesus is not the same thing as God. He was, they argued, of another substance than God.

Others took an altogether different view. They maintained that Jesus was both fully God and fully human; that he was God come down in human flesh, God with us, Emmanuel, the same substance as God himself.

As Arius and his supporters argued their position at length, the assembled bishops listened respectfully. But as Arius continued with some force, legend has it that Nicholas became more and more agitated. Finally, he could bear it no longer. Outraged, he got up, crossed the room and slapped Arius across the face.

For this, he was stripped, beaten and imprisoned, only to be released after the meeting finished. In the end, the Council of Nicaea decided against Arius and declared his view heresy.

But the question debated at Nicaea remains as live and as vital today as it did then.

Who is Jesus?

There are many people who still push, in various forms, the argument advocated by Arius, in essence, that Jesus was no more than a good man. A few years ago, the novelist Philip Pullman published a book entitled *The Good Man Jesus and the Scoundrel Christ*, a work entirely based on this conceit, and one in a long line of volumes that suggest Jesus was just a man.

In 2006, Professor Richard Dawkins was photographed sporting a T-shirt bearing the emblem 'Atheists for Jesus'. The reasoning behind the T-shirt ran that yes, Jesus existed as a historical figure born two thousand years ago, that he lived, taught, did some good stuff and then died. End of story.

But in answering the question, 'Who is Jesus?' I am persuaded less by the fashion sense of Professor Dawkins or the storytelling of Philip Pullman – or indeed the wisdom of either of these great men – than I am swayed by a child called Myriam.

Myriam is an Iraqi Christian, whose family had to flee their home near Mosul when ISIS took control of their town in mid 2014. They fled to Erbil in the relatively safe area in the autonomous region of Kurdistan, where they lived as refugees. Erbil is about 1,500 km from Myra.

Myriam was interviewed that Christmas by Sat-7 Kids, a Christian satellite TV channel. During one part of the interview – carried out in the midst of the refugee camp – the interviewer asks Myriam if she ever thinks that Jesus might have forsaken her.

'No,' answers Myriam, 'sometimes I cry because we left our home, but I'm not angry at God … even if we're suffering here. He provides for us.'

Myriam tells the interviewer she and her family have very little. She misses school and particularly her best friend.

This young child is powerless and homeless in a country at war. And yet what comes across is not what Myriam does not have, but rather what she is in possession of: a deep and joyous belief that Jesus Christ is God.

At the end of the interview, Myriam sings a song of her own choice – and it's a song of praise to Christ.

How joyful is the day on which I believed in Christ.
My joy was made complete at dawn and I sang with
    gratitude:
a new life, a joyful day,
my love to my glorious saviour, day by day will it
    grow.[2]

Myriam knows the answer to the question of who Jesus is. It's the same as St Nicholas of Myra's.

Questions for reflection

1 What are the consequences of the story of St Nicholas being lost to Santa Claus? Is the Dutch commentator Wim Kunst correct in suggesting that 'Santa Claus is becoming too popular and it is the Americanization of our society that people are afraid of'?

2 What opportunities are available to the Church – and wider culture – to reclaim St Nicholas from Santa Claus? Does the plight of refugee children offer such a chance?

3 Look up and watch Myriam's interview with Sat-7 Kids: https://www.youtube.com/watch?v=_ige6CcXuMg. What strikes you about her message?

Thursday 7
St Ambrose of Milan

Today the Church commemorates St Ambrose of Milan who was born around AD 339 in what is now Trier, Germany. The son of a Roman official of Gaul, Ambrose followed in his father's footsteps and became a public official, serving as Governor of Aemilia-Liguria. Tradition holds that, following the death of Auxentius, Bishop of Milan, in 374, Ambrose attended the church meeting called to appoint a new bishop with the intention (in his official capacity) of keeping the peace between factions. Instead, he himself was called upon by the meeting to be the new bishop, a role he reluctantly accepted.

Whenever I think of Ambrose, I am reminded of a story I once heard as part of a sermon preached on his commemoration almost twenty years ago.

The tale, reminiscent of C. S. Lewis's *The Screwtape Letters*, begins with the devil paying a visit to two of his trainee demons to see how they were getting on in their trade of tempting humans into sin.

As he happens upon his minions in the middle of the desert, the devil discovers that his two trainees are in a state of frustration and despair.

'How goes it?' asks the devil.

'Absolutely terrible,' replies one of the junior demons.

'It's this saint. We just can't get to him,' continues the other. 'Every day he stands on that pole in the middle of the desert, fixing his mind on God. From dawn till dusk he stands there, meditating, praying, worshipping and at peace. We have tried everything to stop him: lustful thoughts, fantasies, distractions, whatever we do he doesn't respond. He just stands there, balancing on that pole, completely serene, communing with God.'

'Ah, I see,' replies the devil. 'He's one of those. Leave this to me.'

The devil approached the man and started whispering in his ear.

All of a sudden, the man began to shout out. Clearly infuriated, his face contorted, he started to wobble unsteadily before falling off the stone pole on which he had been standing.

The devil sauntered back to his trainees, a picture of proud insouciance.

The trainees were awestruck.

'How did you do that?' they asked, amazed. 'What did you say?'

'Oh, I simply told him that his brother had just been made Bishop of Milan,' the devil replied.

'Is that it?' asked one of the junior devils. 'Is that all? How did that change anything?'

'The thing about humans,' Satan replied, 'is that they just cannot cope with what they see as undeserved reward. This man knows all his brother's faults and conceits, remembers his past sins and knows how flawed he is. Just the thought of him becoming a bishop tears at his soul. He cannot stand even the thought of it.'

The devil winks at his trainees, pats them both on the back and leaves them to continue their work.

There was no suggestion in the sermon that this story was connected to Ambrose per se, despite the reference to Milan. For although Ambrose was the youngest of three siblings and his rise to the episcopal ranks was unprecedented – he was baptised, deaconed, priested and made a bishop in just over a week – his writing, preaching and teaching led him to be considered one of the four doctors of the Western Church, alongside St Gregory the Great, St Jerome and St Augustine of Hippo, in whose life and faith Ambrose played a key role. Celebrated for his scholarship, musicianship, service to the poor, oratory and as a defender of the Church and its faith, whatever favour Ambrose received, it is unlikely that it was considered undeserved.

But there remains a truth in this tale told of the devil. People continue to struggle with the concept of grace. Unwarranted favour being shown to the undeserving seems to offend our natural sensibilities.

We hear it in the voice of the psalmist who complains to God in Psalm 73 about the good things that happen to bad people: 'For I envied the arrogant when I saw the prosperity of the wicked … in vain I have kept my heart pure and have washed my hands in innocence' (vv. 7, 13).

And it isn't just the psalmist. Counted among people who struggle with what we see as 'unfairness' are those of us who believe that our salvation comes, not through anything we ourselves have earned, but rather through the life, death and resurrection of Jesus Christ. So we are called both to recognise the grace that we depend on in our own lives and to extend grace to others, not only to those who we think deserving of it, but especially – particularly – to those we think do not merit such love. Jesus was clear about this in the Sermon on the Mount:

> 'You have heard that it was said, "Love your neighbour and hate your enemy." But I tell you, love your enemies and pray for those who persecute you, that you may be children of your Father in heaven. He causes his sun to rise on the evil and the good, and sends rain on the righteous and the unrighteous.'
> (Matthew 5:43–5)

As we begin our Advent journey, it is worth reminding ourselves that we are sinners redeemed, recipients of a grace we have done nothing to earn or deserve. We are called to be mindful of this grace God has shown to us, to be penitent, but also to be generous to those who, like us, are invited to share in the riches of Christ.

We are called to give to others what has been given to us in abundance: mercy, overflowing forgiveness and wondrous grace.

Questions for reflection

1 Have you ever felt like the man on the top of the pole in the story? Can you think of occasions when you have reacted strongly to the 'undeserved' flourishing of someone you know or have read about?

2 What does it take to genuinely wish such a person well or to remain at peace when you see or hear of them flourishing? How can we nurture such a heart attitude?

3 Harrowing as they are, consider looking up the reports of the court statements of the relatives of those killed in the Emmanuel AME Church in Charleston in 2015: https://www.youtube.com/watch?v=0uNZy5AwOTA. What do these reports arouse within you?

Friday 8

Revelation 7:9–12: before the throne of God

After this I looked, and there before me was a great multitude that no one could count, from every nation, tribe, people and language, standing before the throne and before the Lamb. They were wearing white robes and were holding palm branches in their hands. And they cried out in a loud voice:

'Salvation belongs to our God,
who sits on the throne,
and to the Lamb.'

All the angels were standing round the throne and round the elders and the four living creatures. They fell down on their faces before the throne and worshipped God, saying:

'Amen!
Praise and glory
and wisdom and thanks and honour
and power and strength
be to our God for ever and ever.
Amen!'

On 26 July 2022, 635 bishops of the Anglican Communion and 464 spouses travelled to Canterbury for the fifteenth

Lambeth Conference. Its theme was 'God's Church for God's World – Walking, Listening and Witnessing Together'.

Usually, the Lambeth Conference takes place every 10 years, and the previous one had been in 2008. However, the Covid pandemic and other issues contributed to a four-year delay.

The Anglican Communion represents approximately 85 million people in more than 165 countries worldwide, speaking more than 2,000 languages, across some 500 different cultures. It is a vast and diverse family which points to that picture of heaven in the book of Revelation, especially during worship, and particularly during the Lord's Prayer.

You may well have been in a service where there's been an instruction to pray the Lord's Prayer in 'your first language' or 'in whatever language you are most comfortable with'. In my experience, this has often led to a splattering of European or Asian languages being heard in a predominantly English-language environment. But in Canterbury Cathedral at the Lambeth Conference, the invitation to pray the Lord's Prayer in indigenous languages led to the most glorious and uplifting sound. There was no way of telling which language predominated and nor did it matter. The sound that came forth was not a confused babble but a united chorus of praise – united not by linguistics but by the common lifting up of hearts. Each time we prayed together as a gathered body, I was left lost for words … I can hardly describe the sheer joy and privilege of being part of the multitude praising God in different languages, from all tribes and nations.

Barely two weeks prior to the start of the Lambeth Conference, I had been consecrated as a bishop at a service in York Minster. So, although I had been to the 2008 conference as a member of staff and knew something of what to expect, there was little doubt that in terms of time served I was, more than probably, the most inexperienced bishop present.

When I mentioned how recently I'd been ordained to one fellow attendee, he joked I should be wearing an L-plate to make my newness plain to all concerned, while another bishop (who had been consecrated for more than twenty years) greeted me each morning at breakfast with the cry, 'Here comes the baby bishop!' But my newness proved to be no barrier to conversation, fellowship and prayer.

While the business within centred around the ten 'Lambeth calls', outside the conference media conversations were dominated by the issue of sexuality and reports of disagreement. There were moments – particularly around the call on Human Dignity and Sexuality – where the conversation overlapped, but for the most part, the topics of sex and sexuality were absent from the discussions and Bible studies in which I participated or of which I was part. This may have been partly the consequence of some churches in the Communion staying away from the conference, citing the issue of sexuality as the reason for their non-attendance. This absence was grievous and stressed that a part of the body was missing, but it also served to emphasise the commitment of others who had taken the decision to be there, despite incentives to the contrary.

If gathering together for prayer and worship from different tribes and nations was the highlight, a low point was discovering from other bishops what they had forsaken in order to attend. In conversation it became clear that provinces, mainly from Africa, were offered financial inducements by church organisations in wealthier parts of the world if they agreed to boycott the conference, or were threatened with penalties if they did not. One bishop was told that, if his province attended, they would lose a year's worth of diesel funding for their transport. Another that, if they attended, they would not receive promised resources for church growth. Another was told of what additional resources might be on offer if they announced a boycott and stayed at home. In all three cases, the bishops took the costly decision to ignore the inducements and to forsake the promised financial backing in order to come.

It was a sad irony that at the very conference where we were celebrating the togetherness of God's people and pointing to that image before God's throne, we were also discovering a fresh division at work in the body of Christ: a new neo-colonialism where financial inducement and reward was being used by richer countries to control the poor.

I left Canterbury inspired by those with whom I had spent time: the bishop whose diocese was in effect a refugee camp; the bishop who had been exiled from his country for speaking out about the dictatorial regime and had not seen his wife or children for four years; the bishop who, even during the conference itself, spoke out about the actions of the government in his province to damage churches and invade holy sites.

Justin Welby summed things up perfectly during one of his keynote addresses:

> Whatever else comes out of this Lambeth Conference, at the heart of it must be the deepening and the building of relationships as our first objective ... We need bishops who love God and love people. If you can tick those boxes, the rest doesn't matter very much.

Questions for reflection

1 In the image from Revelation, it seems that English will be a minority language in heaven. Take a moment to think about how that might feel for you.
2 How can we best support those churches and bishops who serve in places of challenge and repression? What proactive steps can we take?
3 Is there ever a justification for withholding funds – or promising additional resources – in order to change someone else's beliefs or doctrinal understanding?

Saturday 9
Helen Berhane

Remember those who are in prison, as though you were
in prison with them; those who are being tortured, as
though you yourselves were being tortured.
(Hebrews 13:3, NRSV)

His Excellency Isaias Afewerki
President of the State of Eritrea
Office of the President
PO Box 257
Asmara
Eritrea

20 March 2006

Dear Excellency

I write as President of the student body of Cranmer Hall at
St John's College in Durham to express my deep concern
for the nation of Eritrea and its treatment of more than
1,800 evangelical Christians.

I understand that many evangelical Christians have
been unjustly imprisoned as a result of exercising their
constitutional right to freedom of religion.

I write to you as president of your great country to
request that the rights of those currently imprisoned be

respected and that they be released forthwith. In the meantime, I would humbly request that each prisoner be granted access to medical treatment and also that you would grant access to these individuals by their families.

With the assurance of my prayers for you as you seek to establish and maintain justice in your country,

Arun Arora

In his address to the bishops of the worldwide Anglican Communion delivered on 24 July 2008 at the Lambeth Conference, the then Prime Minister of the UK, Gordon Brown, spoke these words:

> You know it was said in ancient Rome of Cicero, that when he came to speak at the forum and crowds came to hear him, they turned to one another after he had spoken, and said: great speech. But it was said of Demosthenes in ancient Athens that, when he came to speak and the crowd heard him, they turned to one another and they said: let's march.

The application to preachers is clear: there are those who can preach on a text in a way that will encourage reflection, and there are those whose preaching can inspire action.

I was training for ordained ministry at Cranmer Hall and regularly attending the evening service at Nic's, never for one moment thinking that more than a decade later I would return to serve as its vicar. The speaker that night was David Day, a Demosthenes among preachers, whose books remain key texts on the art. During his sermon, David spoke of the persecution suffered by Christians in Eritrea. The letter reproduced above was written the following morning.

On 22 May 2002, the Eritrean government ordered the closure of all churches not belonging to the Orthodox, Roman Catholic or Lutheran denominations. In the subsequent clampdown, members of minority Christian evangelical churches faced fierce persecution, even though freedom of religion is guaranteed in the Eritrean Constitution.

Amnesty International estimated that 2,000 members of minority churches, including about 20 pastors, were detained in the months that followed. Detainees were held incommunicado in harsh conditions, without charge or trial. Initially imprisoned in police stations, they were subsequently moved to army camps and security prisons in different parts of the country, including the main military training centre at Sawa. Some were held in metal shipping containers and underground cells. One of those detained was Helen Berhane.

Helen started to write songs at the age of 14 and first began to preach at the age of 16, often to crowds of hundreds. Having been raised Orthodox, she later joined the Evangelical Rema Church. She travelled and preached as a young Christian, attracting huge support: 'I remember when I was in Eritrea before the church closed. We had a huge revival, so they arrested the pastor and me,' she said of her church, which at that time had about 4,000 members.

Helen had just released a cassette of gospel music when she was detained in the capital, Asmara, on 13 May 2004.

After her arrest, she was sent to Mai Serwa military camp where conditions were brutal. 'Torture was a part of everyday life,' Helen would later recall, with physical abuse regularly used on occasions when she refused to sign documents recanting or renouncing her faith. On one occasion, after quoting Scripture passages to the guards, she was asked where she was hiding her Bible. When she replied that she was quoting from memory, where many texts were stored, she received several blows to the head in response.

Yet despite the brutality of her treatment, Helen took inspiration from the imprisonment of others, particularly her memory of Paul and Silas in the book of Acts, where they spent time in cells singing praise. Of that period in prison, Helen says,

> I sang from day one, trying to give thanks for all that I had to endure … I remembered the verse from Philippians 4:4 – 'Rejoice in the Lord always' – so I gave thanks: thank you for the cold, thank you for the food, thank you for the maggots in the container in which I was imprisoned.

Helen was often beaten for singing and was further tortured when it was discovered that she had started to preach the gospel to her guards and captors. After one particularly brutal assault, she was sent to hospital where it was discovered she was suffering from a range of injuries including heavy internal bleeding. Helen believes that she was released at this time, after more than two years' detention, so that she did not die in the military camp.

Months of medical treatment followed, and it was years before she could walk again. Initially Helen applied to the UK for asylum and was interviewed by immigration officials at the British High Commission in Khartoum in January 2007. Seven months later, with no decision on her case by the British authorities, she sought help from Denmark, which took one month to determine that she was a genuine asylum seeker.

Today Helen is still working for justice in Eritrea, where religious oppression continues. She has testified internationally and spoken of her plight and the cases of those still imprisoned. Since her release she has addressed the United Nations in Capitol Hill in the USA and also Parliamentarians in the UK.

Helen offers an account of her time in detention in her memoir *Song of the Nightingale*. She writes: 'If I could sing in prison, imagine what you can do for God's glory with your freedom.'[3]

Questions for reflection

1 A number of human rights organisations campaigned for Helen's release, including Amnesty International and Christian Solidarity Worldwide. Both encourage letter writing and emails as part of campaigns for action. Could you write a letter for someone unjustly imprisoned?

2 Have you ever heard a sermon or a talk which has inspired you to act differently? Can you remember why?

3 Helen was recently interviewed on a visit to the UK; the interview can be seen here: https://www.youtube.com/watch?v=UjhIp0oxT5M. In the interview, she speaks of the opportunities to act for God's glory with the freedom that many of us take for granted. What form of action might that take?

The Second Sunday of Advent
Leah Sharibu

On 19 February 2018 at 5.30 pm, 110 schoolgirls aged between 11 and 19 were kidnapped from the Government Girls' Science and Technical College in Dapchi in north-east Nigeria by a terrorist group.

A month later, on 21 March, 104 of the abducted girls were released. The kidnappers advised their parents not to send them to school again and that *boko* ('education') was *haram* ('forbidden') for girls. The advice would be backed up with violence if not heeded.

Of the 6 girls who were not released, it later transpired that 5 had died during their ordeal. Just one of the Dapchi schoolgirls, Leah Sharibu, aged 14 at the time of her capture, remained hostage. Her friends reported that she was a Christian and that she was not released with the other children because she refused to convert to Islam – or, to be more precise, the Salafi jihadist version of the Islamic faith practised by her kidnappers.

Leah's mother Rebecca was said to have fainted after receiving the news that her eldest child was not among those freed: 'My heart was broken … when I searched through the released girls and could not set my eyes on my dear daughter, Leah.' She continued:

To the Boko Haram members, I have nothing to say other than that they should have pity on my only daughter and release her ... I know that, in this world, everyone chooses the path of faith he or she has chosen in worshipping God. There is no way one could be forced to do what he or she does not know. It is not possible.

There were strident appeals and demands that the Federal Government should immediately act to secure Leah's rescue or release. In his response, the Nigerian President Muhammadu Buhari assured the Nigerian Senate that everything would be done to secure this.

A statement by the President's spokesman said:

The Buhari administration will not relent in its efforts to bring Leah Sharibu safely back home to her parents, as it has done for the other girls, after she was held back by the terrorists over her decision, as reported, not to convert from Christianity to Islam. President Buhari is fully conscious of his duty under the constitution to protect all Nigerians, irrespective of faith, ethnic background or geopolitical location and will not shirk in this responsibility. President Buhari assures the Sharibu family that he will continue to do all he can to ensure that they also have cause to rejoice with their daughter soon.

That was five years ago.

Since their daughter's kidnap, the Sharibu family have consistently issued calls for prayer from all Christians to enable their daughter's freedom. Speaking with reporters, Mrs Sharibu said:

> She is not with us and all we can do is fast and pray for her as a family, and I want to appeal to all Nigerians and other concerned people around the world to help us pray for her safety, wherever she is, and for her return as well. President Buhari seemed to have forgotten about Leah, but we know that God who brought her forth will not forget her. We believe that God is keeping watch over her and our prayers would be answered.

Leah's plight has become representative of that of thousands of young girls in Nigeria. The Nigerian *Guardian* newspaper named her as their person of the year in 2018, stating:

> She has since become the symbol of Nigeria's refusal to give in to agents of darkness, hell-bent on dividing the country and appropriating a section of the nation's territory unto themselves. She turned down personal liberty and chose to put her life on the line so that the whole of Nigeria may fulfil the promise of freedom and prosperity. She is a true heroine.[1]

In January 2020, news outlets reported that Leah had given birth to a baby boy after being forcibly married off to a Boko Haram commander. The news of a second child's arrival was reported at the end of 2020.

Her captors declared her a 'slave for life'.

Speaking to a journalist in 2021, Leah's mother was asked: 'Do you have hope that you will see Leah again?' Rebecca answered: 'Yes, by the grace of God. I have not lost hope because God is in control and people are praying. I have the hope that one day, I will see my daughter again.'

The German theologian Karl Barth is reputed to have said that the clasping of hands in prayer is the beginning of an uprising against the disorder of the world. During my time at St Nic's in Durham, we prayed for Leah over the past five years. We signed petitions, wrote letters and emails. We joined with others in calling for her release. Leah's name is still placed on the church's prayer sheet every week.

The season of Advent is a time of waiting and wrestling with the darkness. We look for the coming of Christ into the world – the light that shines in the darkness – with expectation and hope. 'O Come, O come Emmanuel,' we sing, 'and ransom captive Israel.'

Unlike Helen Berhane, at the time of writing Leah Sharibu remains in captivity. But the call for her freedom continues. This Advent, may we join our prayers with those across the world in praying for the release of Leah Sharibu and for Leah's family as they wait, and to pray for all who are held captive for their faith. May we clasp our hands in hope and expectation of the coming of the year of the Lord's favour, when there shall be freedom for the prisoners and the oppressed shall be set free.

Questions for reflection

1 Proverbs 13:12 famously states that 'hope deferred makes the heart sick'. How do you engage with the process of waiting?

2 The second part of the proverb says 'that a longing fulfilled is a tree of life'. What changes with waiting?

3 Leah Sharibu is one of many held in captivity for their faith. In addition to praying, what else might you do to enable her freedom?

Monday 11
Asia Bibi

If I speak in the tongues of men or of angels, but do
not have love ...
(1 Corinthians 13:1)

How do we measure love?

It's the kind of question that's often a subject for wedding
sermons. The minister might reflect on the Apostle Paul's
hymn to love in 1 Corinthians 13, or perhaps on another
favourite text from the Song of Songs:

Place me like a seal over your heart,
   like a seal on your arm;
for love is as strong as death,
   its jealousy unyielding as the grave.
It burns like blazing fire,
   like a mighty flame.
Many waters cannot quench love;
   rivers cannot sweep it away.
If one were to give
   all the wealth of one's house for love,
   it would be utterly scorned.
(8:6–7)

Of course, love comes in different forms. C. S. Lewis famously wrote about four loves of which Eros (romantic love)

is but one. Beyond romance, there is the self-giving love that does not count the cost but is rooted in and enriched by the gospel. For Jesus, this kind of love was measured not so much in hearts and roses but sacrifice: 'Greater love has no one than this: to lay down one's life for one's friends' (John 15:13).

Through the centuries, there have been countless examples of Christian women and men who have surrendered their lives for their friends, for their faith and for one another. We will never know the names of all of those who have done so, but we can remember and honour those whose love and courage has led to the ultimate sacrifice.

Asia Bibi's troubles began in June 2009 in her village, Ittan Wali, a patchwork of lush fields and dusty streets in rural Punjab, Pakistan. Asia lived with her husband and children, and hers was the only Christian household in the village. One day while picking berries, a disagreement developed between Asia and other women over sharing water. Days later, these women claimed she had insulted the Prophet Muhammad. The dispute escalated quickly and soon Asia was being pursued by a mob. 'In the village, they tried to put a noose around my neck, so that they could kill me,' she said.

The police were called. After removing Asia and her family from the village, they charged her with blasphemy on the basis of the accusations made. She was imprisoned for more than a year while awaiting trial. In November 2010, Asia Bibi was convicted of blasphemy and sentenced to death.

The severity of the punishment and the disputed nature of events meant that the case garnered both national and international attention. The imam at the village mosque was reported as saying he cried with joy when the death sentence was passed on Asia Bibi. He helped to bring the case against her, and when questions of pardon arose, he was resolute in his view that she would be made to pay, one way or another. 'If the law punishes someone for blasphemy, and that person is pardoned, then we will also take the law in our hands,' he said. One radical cleric promised 500,000 Pakistani rupees to anyone prepared to 'finish her'. He suggested that the Taliban might be happy to do so.

Over the Christmas period, political parties were out on the streets protesting about the case, threatening anarchy if Asia Bibi were freed, or if there was any attempt to amend the blasphemy law.

Some public figures came out in her defence, including the Governor of the Punjab region in Pakistan, Salman Taseer, who suggested that the law was outdated and being used to settle scores against Christians on matters wholly unrelated to religion.

On 4 January 2011, as he was returning to his car after meeting a friend for lunch, one of Taseer's bodyguards, Malik Qadri, shot him 26 times with a sub-machine gun. The bodyguard then threw his weapon down and put his hands up when one of his colleagues aimed at him. He reportedly pleaded to be arrested. Qadri stated that he killed Taseer due to his vocal opposition to the blasphemy law in Pakistan.

One of those who protested most vocally about the assassination of Salman Taseer was the Pakistan Government's Minister for Minorities, Shahbaz Bhatti.

Mr Bhatti, himself a Christian, also spoke out on behalf of Asia Bibi, arguing that she should win her appeal against her conviction, or be pardoned by the President of Pakistan. He argued that Asia Bibi was one of dozens of innocent people who were accused every year under the blasphemy law. As a result of his vocal support for Asia Bibi, Shahbaz Bhatti received numerous death threats. He spoke about these during a television interview with Al Jazeera at the end of February 2011:

> The forces of violence want to impose their radical philosophy in Pakistan ... Whoever stands against them is threatened. I want to share that I believe in Jesus Christ who has given his own life for us. I know the meaning of the cross and I am a follower of the cross. I am ready to die for a cause. I am living for my community and suffering people and I will die to defend their rights. These threats cannot change my principles. I would prefer to die for my principles and the justice of my community rather than to compromise for these threats.

Less than a week after this interview, on 2 March, Shahbaz Bhatti was assassinated. According to the BBC, he was travelling to work through a residential district, having just left his mother's home, when his vehicle was sprayed with bullets. Bhatti was taken to a nearby hospital but was pronounced dead on arrival. The group Tehrik-i-Taliban told the BBC that they carried out the attack, because Bhatti was a 'known blasphemer'.

In October 2018, after eight years' imprisonment, much of which was spent in solitary confinement due to the threats to her life, Asia Bibi was released when Pakistan's Supreme Court overturned her conviction. That decision prompted protests from religious hardliners calling for her death and demanding that the government prevent her from leaving Pakistan. Seven months later, Asia Bibi left the country and arrived in Canada.

During her imprisonment, Asia Bibi learned of the international outcry over her detention and the prayers of Christians across the globe. She also recalled her sorrow at hearing while in jail that two politicians who tried to help her had been murdered. 'I cried a lot. I cried for more than a week for them. Even today, my heart is full of sadness for them and I miss them,' she said.

In an interview with the BBC, she recounted:

They said change your faith, and you'll be freed. But I said no. I will live my sentence. With my faith. I found out from my husband that the whole world was praying for me. And that even the Pope had prayed for me. That made me happy. And I found out the whole world was praying for my misery to end. That made me feel that their prayers would definitely free me.

Questions for reflection

1 Salman Taseer and Shahbaz Bhatti were murdered for speaking out publicly for Asia Bibi. What difference does it make (if any) that one was Muslim the other a Christian?

2 Watch Shahbaz Bhatti's final interview with Al Jazeera: https://www.youtube.com/watch?v=oBTBqUJomRE. What strikes you most about the interview?

3 How do *you* measure love?

Tuesday 12
The Revd Canon Jemima Prasadam

There are more than a thousand portraits of clerics and preachers to be found in the National Portrait Gallery's collection. They variously include Thomas Cranmer, Cardinal Wolsey, Jonathan Swift, Michael Ramsey and a host of others. The vast majority are painted portraits, but among some of the more recent commissions are photographic studies, such as those of Lucy Winkett, Alice Goodman and my favourite one of all, Jemima Prasadam.

Next to her portrait by the West Midlands-based photographer Lorentz Gullachsen is a description of the sitter that reads:

Jemima Prasadam (1940–), priest

She was born in Andhra Pradesh in southern India; British missionaries had converted her grandfather to Christianity. She immigrated to Great Britain in 1975 to help spread the Christian message. When the Anglican Church admitted female priests for the first time in 1987, Prasadam became the first non-white woman to be ordained. She is vicar for the multi-faith and multi-racial parish of Lozells, an inner-city area widespread with unemployment and poverty in west Birmingham. An active member of the community, she delivers services, chairs meetings, visits the sick and helps to run playgroups. She firmly believes that 'our mission here is to bring up our children with dignity to play their part in this community and this country'.

Jemima, or 'Aunty Jemima' as she is more fondly known, was the first Indian priest I ever met. As the vicar of St Paul and St Silas in Lozells from 1996 to 2014, she brought her own inimitable style and personality to her parish. Standing barely five feet tall and dressed in her sari and dog collar, Aunty Jemima was a familiar figure to those in Lozells and beyond. When I was getting married, and I decided not to have any form of Hindu ceremony as part of my wedding, it was Aunty Jemima who came to spend time with my mother and family as we navigated the cultural and religious contours that came with being a Christian in an Indian household.

The Index of Multiple Deprivation still lists Lozells as among the country's top 5% of most deprived wards, with the area known for riots in 1985 and 2005. Such depth of need could be overwhelming for those called to serve in such parishes. But where some might see challenge, Jemima spotted opportunity. One thing she became involved in was befriending asylum seekers who had been housed in Lozells as a designated dispersal area.

We had many of these women and men from the Democratic Republic of Congo who were in a new place, not knowing anyone and often quite bewildered. But they knew French as their first language and we had lots of school children in the area who were doing French at school but needed help. So we started an after-school club in church where those new to the area could find a welcome and meet people, while also helping out the children with their French language and conversation.

While such a creative and agile response to community need highlighted Jemima's ability to respond to changing circumstance, it was her gift as an everyday evangelist that marked her out and enabled her to draw together the disparate parts of her community.

This found its form in what she referred to as 'bus-stop theology', which she put into action along the half-mile route from her vicarage to the church of St Paul and St Silas. The six bus stops she passed in her daily walk to church each provided an opportunity for conversation.

In a post-retirement interview with the *Church Times*, Jemima reflected on her ability to speak of God naturally, in the way most native Brits would speak of the weather:

I don't go out looking to talk to people, but I am ready to do it. I don't pass anybody without saying 'Hello', and when I leave, I always say 'God bless you'. Meetings happen on a daily basis, but often only last as long as it takes for the bus to arrive.

There is no set pattern: it is spontaneous. People are perhaps reading a newspaper. I ask is there anything good, and they usually come out with something. Some people are very British and reserved, but most people are prepared to talk. They often say they are not religious, but I say we are all spiritual beings and they agree; so I simply tell them that weak and simple people like me call that God.[2]

Given that there were both Christians and Hindus in her own family in India, it is not surprising that interfaith matters formed a daily part of Jemima's work. Her relations with the Pandit of the Hindu temple across from the vicarage were as warm as they were with leaders of the Sikh and Muslim communities in the area. And as a woman priest, she provided a surprising role model for other women and girls in the area. One group of Muslim schoolgirls would refer to her as the Hafiza – a feminised version of a Hafiz – someone who has memorised the Qur'an by heart and is treated with honour.

While it was for her interfaith work that Jemima Prasadam was awarded an MBE in 2005, it was her inspirational work in the community that she loved and cared for that led to her story featuring as part of the 'faith zone' in the Millennium Dome at the turn of the century. Yet I suspect these moments of pride pale in comparison with the joy she would have experienced in March of this year, when one of her daughters, Smitha Prasadam, was announced as the next Bishop of Huddersfield in the diocese of Leeds.

Now retired and settled in the leafy suburbs of Richmond in south-west London, Jemima's remarkable ministry continues to flourish and she remains every bit the everyday evangelist. Her rare and disarming gift of making those from every walk of life feel seen, connected and respected is still to the fore, and her bus-stop theology as vibrant as ever.

Questions for reflection

1 How easy do you find it to talk about your faith? Does doing so feel markedly different from chatting about the weather?
2 It has been suggested that faith is 'always personal but never private'. What do you understand by this?
3 The Church is often the main driver of interfaith partnerships in the UK. How much value do we place on this ministry?

Wednesday 13
St Lucy of Syracuse

As a vicar dealing with the financial challenges of running a parish, I was somewhat surprised to discover that the official policy of the Church of England on individual giving is that church members are encouraged to commit only 5% of their net income to the Church and a further 5% to other charities. My Christian upbringing in the Baptist tradition meant that my understanding of the biblical concept of a tithe was that you gave 10% of your income to the Church. If you wanted to give more, either to the Church or to other charities, that was fine but 10% to the Church was the baseline. I naturally thought this would apply in the Church of England too.

In the places where I served, there were always people who gave sacrificially, often much more than 10%. Earlier in the history of St Nic's, when the church needed to be completely reordered, some people cancelled holidays in order to offer what was needed, while some remortgaged their houses. These were people who took to heart the understanding in the thanksgiving prayer that 'all things come from you and from your own do we give you'.[3]

Giving is an intensely personal business. Like many vicars, I made it a point of principle never to know who gave what to church. Fundamentally, giving is part of discipleship and an individual's relationship with God. If people are going to short-change what they offer to God, they will be answerable to someone much more important than the vicar. The account in the book of Acts about Ananias and Sapphira withholding money is a cautionary tale.

The Bible mentions money a great deal and it is something that Jesus consistently addresses in his parables and teachings, as with the widow giving all that she has to live on to the temple treasury; the parable of Dives and Lazarus; the sadness of the rich young ruler; or the warning to give to the poor discreetly so your left hand does not know what your right hand is doing. There is a clear caution against pride and avarice, and encouragement towards generosity. Rarely do we hear about those punished for giving away too much.

Today the Church commemorates St Lucy, also known as Lucia of Syracuse. Lucy was born in AD 283 in Syracuse, Sicily. According to legend – much of which is disputed – her father died when she was young and, in order to secure her daughter's future, Lucy's mother arranged for her to be married to the son of a wealthy pagan family. After the miraculous cure of her mother from illness, Lucy persuaded her mother to allow her to distribute her dowry and other goods to the poor. Upon discovering this, the young man became outraged by Lucy's generosity with money that he thought to be his property and reported her to the Governor of the region. Lucy's crime was not the giving away but rather the faith that inspired this, a faith illegal under the law. This was the time of the Diocletian persecution when Roman authorities were attempting to re-establish cult worship, not least of the emperor himself. According to some accounts, upon discovering that Lucy was a Christian, the Governor of Syracuse ordered her to burn a sacrifice to the image of Diocletian as penance. Lucy refused. The governor ordered her death and she died in 304 at the age of 21.

The oldest record of Lucy's martyrdom was written in the fifth century. By the sixth century, her story was sufficiently widespread that, according to the Venerable Bede, she was being commemorated with a holy day in England. Despite this, it is thought that only two Church of England churches have Lucy as their patron saint, one in Shropshire, where the attached primary school also bears her name, and the other in Lincolnshire.

Lucy's legend celebrates her commitment to the faith and her refusal to deny it. As a martyr, she became an exemplar of the many who suffered as a result of the last and most severe persecutions of Christians in the Roman Empire, which lasted for a decade. In Latin, Lucy's name means 'light', and with her feast day falling in December on the shortest day of the Julian calendar, she became associated with the coming of the one true light. In Sweden, the Lucia celebrations mark the presence of light on the longest night and are accompanied by Lucia songs:

The night treads heavily
around yards and dwellings
In places unreached by sun,
the shadows brood.
Into our dark house she comes,
bearing lighted candles,
Saint Lucia, Saint Lucia.[4]

By the time of medieval accounts, additional details began to be attached to the legend, including the order for Lucy to be burned being frustrated by wood that would not ignite, and Lucy's eyes being gouged out as a consequence of her denouncing the Governor and pronouncing that the death of the emperor would come soon.

Yet none of these later additions is as strange as what actually occurred in November 1981 at the Church of St Jeremiah in Venice. Two gunmen burst into the church and ordered the parish priest and a visiting honeymoon couple to lie on the floor while they seized St Lucy's mummified skeleton from its heavy glass-enclosed crypt and put it in a sack. The bizarre nature of the robbery was underscored when, during the theft of the body, the saint's head broke off at the neck and rolled away on the floor. The silver death mask which had covered her face was left behind.

According to the local magistrate, police investigations focused on a local criminal who was suspected of involvement in a recent kidnapping and murder of a restaurant owner. 'Our investigations indicate that the robbers did not steal the bones for ransom but to make other demands on the authorities,' the magistrate said. He did not disclose what the other demands were.

A month later, on the feast day of St Lucy itself, the mummified remains were discovered by the police in a bag at a hunting lodge just outside Venice. After the remains were tested as authentic, they were taken back to the church where the Vicar General of Venice presided over a brief ceremony to celebrate St Lucy's return.

Questions for reflection

1 Are you surprised by the recommended figure of 5% giving to the Church? Does this seem too low?

2 Only two churches are named after Lucy. Why do you think Lucy's memory has largely been forgotten in the UK? What might it be about her story that fails to resonate?

3 How does Lucy's story fit into the wider themes of Advent?

Thursday 14

St John of the Cross

The season of Lent is a time of waiting, reflection and preparation. In its last days, we enter into the Passion of Christ, experiencing the darkness of Good Friday and Holy Saturday before the glorious breaking of the Easter dawn.

The theme of waiting for the light is one Lent shares with Advent, as each week candles are lit to anticipate the coming of Christ into the world.

The first, which we lit two weeks ago, is the candle of hope. It is a reminder of the promises God made to the nation of Israel – of the Christ who would come as God takes human flesh and enters into human history. The candle also reminds us of the further promise to be fulfilled. As the Methodist pastor Walter Wink wrote: 'Hope imagines the future and acts as if that hope is irresistible.'[5]

The invitation to each of us is not to ignore the reality of the darkness but to acknowledge it, to confront it with the light that shines in the darkness, which the darkness cannot extinguish.

So, in both Lent and Advent, questions relating to the reality of encountering darkness, to banishment and abandonment, are answered by a promised hope, rooted in the coming of the kingdom of God, inaugurated by the resurrection and completed in Christ's return. But, of course, there can be no Easter Day without Good Friday, no resurrection without crucifixion. In the space in between we wait.

The Old Testament theologian Walter Brueggemann writes that Christians are 'in-betweeners'. We inhabit the space between the cross and the empty tomb, symbolised by Holy Saturday; within that space, we have neither completely escaped the despair of Good Friday nor reached the glory of Easter Day: 'Jesus and his people always live between the banishment of Friday and the gathering of Sunday, always between the exile of crucifixion and the new community of resurrection.'[6]

This experience of remaining faithful in times of darkness is perhaps most famously described by St John of the Cross in his writings on the dark night of the soul. St John was born Juan de Yepes y Álvarez, in Fontiveros, Ávila, Spain in 1542. He studied theology and philosophy at the University of Salamanca before becoming a priest in 1567. Soon afterwards, he encountered Teresa of Ávila, a nun seeking to renew her devotion to poverty, prayer and simplicity in the Carmelite Order.

In 1572, John travelled to Ávila at the invitation of Teresa to become her confessor and spiritual guide. While there, he had a mystical vision of Christ and made a sketch that exists to this day called 'Christ from Above'. Drawing our gaze downwards, the little illustration shows Christ on the cross, and became the inspiration for Salvador Dalí's iconic 1951 painting, *Christ of Saint John of the Cross*.

A dispute among the Carmelite Order led to John's imprisonment in Toledo, and this is where he wrote some of his finest poetry, including 'Noche oscura del alma' ('Dark Night of the Soul'). In this poem, he describes that part of the spiritual journey where God seems silent and the soul abandoned, with the individual suffering from the conviction that 'God has rejected it, and with abhorrence cast it into darkness'. But what feels like abandonment is far from it. The painful sense of being rejected by God is actually a purging of the senses and spirit that prepares the way for an 'inflow of God into the soul'.[7]

John died on 14 December 1591 and was canonised by Pope Benedict XIII in 1726. He is the patron saint of contemplatives, mystics and Spanish poets.

In more recent times the experience of the dark night of the soul was laid bare most strikingly with the publication in 2007 of *Come Be My Light*, the collection of Mother Teresa's private letters to and from her closest spiritual confidants. The book revealed the depth of the abandonment and spiritual dryness that Mother Teresa had battled with over decades.

In one of her letters, she writes:

The place of God in my soul is blank – There is no God in me.
In the darkness … Lord, my God, who am I that You should forsake me? …
The one You have thrown away as unwanted – unloved.
I call, I cling,
I want – and there is no One to answer – no One on Whom I can cling; no, No One. Alone. The darkness is so dark – and I am alone.[8]

The bleakness experienced by John of the Cross and Mother Teresa is not theirs alone. But for both of them, that sense was accompanied by the knowledge that ultimately such abandonment, though it might be expressed through an outpouring of desolation and despair, would find its resolution in a deeper dependency on God. At Advent, the dark night gives way to the cry of the child in the manger; it is burned away by the light of Christ coming into the world.

Writing almost four hundred years after John of the Cross – and also from a prison cell after his arrest in 1943 – Dietrich Bonhoeffer noted:

> The celebration of Advent is possible only to those who are troubled in soul, who know themselves to be poor and imperfect, and who look forward to something greater to come. The Advent season is a season of waiting, but our whole life is an Advent season, that is, a season of waiting for the last Advent, for the time when there will be a new heaven and a new earth.[9]

Questions for reflection

1 Do you recognise the description of the dark night of the soul as expressed by St John of the Cross? Have you experienced your own dark night?
2 Do you agree with Bonhoeffer's assessment of Advent being most meaningful to those who are troubled in soul and waiting?
3 For what are you waiting? Are you ready for Christ to come again?

Friday 15
George Floyd

'Never read the comments beneath your columns. There be dragons.' This sage advice was pressed upon me by a newspaper features editor at one of the papers I wrote for as an occasional columnist. On the whole, it was advice I followed, but there were occasions when, having looked up an article in order to share it on social media, I began to scroll down to view what was written beneath.

One of those times was after I had written a piece about a government minister who had come out in defence of football fans who booed players for taking the knee at the start of football games. Arguing that those who booed were expressing a legitimate freedom of speech, the minister said, 'If people choose to express their view in a particular way, that should always be respected' – a remark which the campaign group Kick It Out described as 'providing shelter to racists'.[10]

Eight comments appeared beneath the article, most of which agreed with the minister's approach. One anonymous comment in particular (vocal keyboard warriors often hide their faces) caught my attention. It read:

Black Lives Matter would have a lot more support if they hadn't hung their banner on the George Floyd case, he was a nasty, violent drug dealing full time criminal, live by the sword etc. There are plenty of law

abiding, hard working black people suffering racism,
why pick this worthless piece of scum?

George Floyd was born on 14 October 1973 in North
Carolina. He was one of five children; his parents separated
w   he was 2 years old, and he moved with his mother
          lifficult neighbourhood in Houston. A promising
          he played both American football and basketball as
          r and obtained a sports scholarship to university
b   pping out. He returned home to a series of short-
te   construction and security before getting into
trou   een 1997 and 2005, he was arrested several
times   and theft charges, spending months in jail. In
August   was arrested and charged with aggravated
robbery   eadly weapon and, after pleading guilty
in 2009, w   nced to five years in prison. It was while
serving his   e that George Floyd turned to Jesus
Christ. Whe   paroled in 2013, he was determined
that his newfo   would help him to change his ways.
    'He came ho   his head on right,' said a friend.
    After George   to Cuney Homes in Houston,
he soon became i   with a local church. Its pastor,
Patrick Ngwolo, de   him as 'a person of peace sent
from the Lord that he   e gospel go forward in a place
that I never lived in'.   gwolo was looking for a way to
reach the residents in Cuney Homes and George volun-
teered to be his guide, knocking on doors with the pastor
and using his knowledge of the local community to help
the church with its ministry. A friend from the church said
that George recognised the deep-seated issues in the area

and wanted to help be part of the change. George's words were, 'I love what you're doing. The neighbourhood need it, the community need it, and if y'all about God's business, then that's my business.'

Another friend from church said George was 'radically changed by the gospel, and his mission was empowering other believers to be able to come in and push that gospel forth'.

One of George's particular concerns was gun violence. As someone respected by many of the young men in the area for what he had been through, George would occasionally make videos for social media and post them for those who followed him. In these posts, George spoke of breaking the cycle of violence he saw, and used his influence to assist with discipleship and outreach in the area. In one of his films he says,

> I've got my shortcomings and my flaws and I ain't better than nobody else. But, man, the shootings that's going on, I don't care what 'hood you're from, where you're at, man. I love you and God loves you. Put them guns down.

A local Christian hip-hop artist and friend of Floyd's remarked, 'The things that he would say to young men always referenced that God trumps street culture. I think he wanted to see young men put guns down and have Jesus instead of the streets.'

In February 2017, George moved from Houston to Minneapolis as part of a church discipleship programme that offered men a route to self-sufficiency by changing their environment and helping them to find jobs. Having attended a rehab programme, his first job was as a security guard at the Salvation Army's homeless shelter in the city. A year later, he found work elsewhere while training to work as a truck driver. However, the advent of Covid meant that he became unemployed. He soon caught Covid himself, and it was about a month after his recovery when he went into Cup Foods on 25 May. There he paid for cigarettes with a $20 bill that the clerk thought was fake.

The events that followed became known across the world.

The video of George's arrest went viral.

Derek Chauvin, a Minneapolis police officer, was filmed kneeling on George's neck as he begged for his life. 'I can't breathe, man,' he can be heard saying in the film. 'Please, let me stand. Please, man.' Mr Chauvin kept his knee on George's neck for eight minutes and forty-six seconds. He did not remove it even after George lost consciousness, and it stayed in place for a full minute after paramedics arrived at the scene.

George Floyd was a Christian with a criminal record who struggled with addiction. He campaigned against gun violence and helped many in his community, becoming part of a church seeking to improve the lives of those in need. In death, he brought about a revolution that he could never have foreseen in life. But even in death, it seems George Floyd is not free from judgement by those who will never be able to see the image of Christ in him.

Questions for reflection

1 George Floyd said he was aware of his own shortcomings, even after he came to faith. God was able to work through that brokenness. What can we learn from this?

2 Not all of those we find difficult to love have criminal records. What blinds us to seeing the image of Christ in our neighbour?

3 Given that racism is a sin, what steps might we take, in the church and outside, to embrace righteousness?

Saturday 16
Dr John Sentamu

In the summer of 2006, during my first week working as Director of Communications for the Archbishop of York, Dr John Sentamu came into my office, clearly troubled. The war between Lebanon and Israel was intensifying, with civilians on both sides being forced from their homes as casualties and the death toll increased. Reports and pictures filled the news. Like many others, Dr Sentamu had been praying earnestly for peace. 'I feel like my prayers are hitting the ceiling,' he said. 'I have been asking the Holy Spirit what I should do. There is a feeling out there of helplessness. We need to help people to act.' Dr Sentamu was due to go on holiday with his wife Margaret to Salzburg in Austria. A Mozart festival was taking place in honour of the 250th birthday of the town's favourite son, but he felt he could not attend while the war was being fought. 'I just can't go. I am going to have to talk with Margaret.'

The next morning, Dr Sentamu appeared on *Today* on BBC Radio 4 to announce that he would be pitching a tent in York Minster. He would remain there for seven days to pray and fast for peace and highlight the plight of those caught up the conflict.

We have an opportunity to stand up and be counted with those in Israel, Lebanon and Palestine and all over the world who seek after peace. This is what this week will be about, people coming together for one purpose alone – to pray for peace in our troubled world and to pray especially for the Middle East. I will lead every day, on the hour, every hour for seven days and will be inviting people from all over the country to pause for a prayer and light a candle for peace.

Sentamu began his fast and prayer vigil for peace on 13 August 2006. The Precentor of York Minster recalled that

the spiritual temperature was raised day by day. There were more visitors. More people wanted to pray. Many more people sought us out to talk about faith, or doubt, or to open up about their needs and hopes … It was all a cathedral should be.

During the week, thousands of people from near and far came to the Minster to pray with Sentamu, including 10 Holocaust survivors from Ireland, and Muslims from York Mosque. But his action was not without its critics, with one commentator suggesting the vigil would leave Sentamu 'looking like a prize boob' if the war continued unabated. Thankfully, on Wednesday of that week, the guns and missiles fell silent. At the end of the vigil, Sentamu said his tent would remain pitched in York Minster as a symbol of the continuing need for prayer until a UN peacekeeping force was put in place in southern Lebanon. He said: 'I continue to invite people to come and to offer prayers of peace in this place for the Middle East, for our nation and for peace in our own hearts.' The conflict formally ended on 8 September 2006.

I first met Dr John Sentamu when he was announced as the new Bishop of Birmingham in 2002. Barely three months after his installation, I witnessed his ability to place prayer and action at the heart of his ministry, when Charlene Ellis and Letisha Shakespeare were gunned down at a New Year party in Aston. In the months that followed, Sentamu went 'undercover' in the area, going door to door, delivering leaflets appealing for witnesses. Weeks later, he made a public appeal for those with knowledge of the incident to come forward, and gave out his personal telephone number for those too scared to talk to the police. One of the gangs implicated in the shooting got word to him and asked if he was prepared to meet. He agreed before being blindfolded and driven to a place where gang members asked him to guarantee that, if they gave evidence, they would not be identified and would be kept safe. Sentamu did his best to reassure them. Months later, after a trial at Leicester Crown Court, four men were jailed for life for the murder of the girls.

John Tucker Mugabe Sentamu was born weighing little over 4lbs; his parents feared that he would not survive the night, so he was baptised immediately. Educated by English missionaries, Sentamu flourished in school and went on to study law at Makerere University. At the age of 24, he was called to the Bar as an Advocate, before becoming a judge in the Uganda High Court. His first posting was to Gulu in Northern Uganda where he first met Janani Luwum, the then Bishop of Northern Uganda. As an opponent of the regime of Idi Amin, Sentamu was outspoken against the deportation of the Ugandan Asians and then refused to overlook the crimes of one of Amin's family. Defying an order from Amin to deliver a not-guilty verdict, Sentamu was arrested and badly beaten in a state security centre, subsequently describing the experience as 'being kicked around like a human football'. He suffered severe internal injuries and was subsequently prayed for by Keith Sutton, then a tutor at Mukono who was later to become Principal of Ridley Hall and eventually Bishop of Kingston and Lichfield, and who arranged for Sentamu and his wife Margaret to leave Uganda.

Arriving in England in 1974, Sentamu studied for a masters and doctorate at the University of Cambridge and trained for ordination. While he was in Cambridge, Sentamu was given news of the murder of Archbishop Janini Luwum by Idi Amin. He responded by saying, 'You killed my friend, I take his place.' Having been Chaplain to Selwyn College and served his curacy at St Andrew Ham, he became vicar of Tulse Hill and was appointed as Bishop of Stepney in 1996.

Nine years later, Sentamu made history by becoming the Church of England's first black archbishop. In 2006, when he led a mission at the University of Oxford, Sentamu recalled the words of a former archbishop, Michael Ramsey who, during his missions in the Universities of Cambridge, Dublin and Oxford in 1960, spoke of the missionary century that saw the spread of Christian faith in Africa and Asia and compared it to the spiritual decay in England. Ramsey ended his address by saying, 'I should love to think of a black Archbishop of York holding a mission here and telling a future generation of the scandal and the glory of the Church.'

Questions for reflection

1 Dietrich Bonhoeffer famously remarked that 'the future of the Church is in prayer and action'.[11] How do you see the link between prayer and action lived out in the Church today?

2 During a live television interview in 2007, John Sentamu cut up his clerical collar as a protest against the dictatorial regime of Robert Mugabe. He vowed he would not wear it again until Mugabe had been removed from office (which happened ten years later). Where do we see such prophetic actions today?

3 What is your reflection on Michael Ramsey's vision of the twenty-first century as a time when reverse mission will take place and those from former colonies will come to England to evangelise its people?

The Third Sunday of Advent
Cardinal Francis-Xavier Nguyen Van Thuan

Rejoice in the Lord always. I will say it again: Rejoice! Let your gentleness be evident to all. The Lord is near. Do not be anxious about anything, but in every situation, by prayer and petition, with thanksgiving, present your requests to God. And the peace of God, which transcends all understanding, will guard your hearts and your minds in Christ Jesus.
(Philippians 4:4–7)

Today is the third Sunday of Advent, also known in the wider Church traditionally as Gaudete Sunday, the Sunday of Joy. *Gaudete* is the Latin word for 'rejoice' and comes from these verses of Philippians 4: 'Gaudete in Domino semper' – 'Rejoice in the Lord always.'

In his Gaudete Sunday sermon in 2014, Pope Francis said that today was an opportunity for the faithful to take a break from fretting about 'all they still haven't done to prepare for Christmas' and instead to take this day and this time to 'think of all the good things in life God has given you'. The purpose of Gaudete Sunday, Pope Francis urged, was to increase our awareness that in life's difficulties we can always turn to the Lord, and that his presence with us, alongside us, is a great reason for joy. 'Shout with joy, rejoice, rejoice,' he said, 'this is the invitation of this Sunday.'

It was a difficult message to communicate during the second Covid lockdown in December 2020, when many people found the restrictions harder to endure than in the first, the previous March. Cold and dark days, the thought of a disrupted Christmas and a pervading sense of isolation may all have contributed. However, encouragement was to be found in the lives of those who had lived through even worse isolation, trial and adversity and yet somehow managed to flourish. One such person is Cardinal Francis-Xavier Nguyen Van Thuan.

In April 1975, Van Thuan was appointed the Roman Catholic Coadjutor Archbishop of Saigon. Six days later, Saigon fell to the North Vietnamese army, and Van Thuan was arrested for his faith and detained by the Communist government. He spent the next thirteen years in prisons and 're-education' camps, including nine in solitary confinement.

During those years, Cardinal Van Thuan began using scraps of paper to compose messages of hope to the people of his diocese and these were smuggled out by fellow prisoners and sympathetic prison guards. More than a thousand of the notes were later assembled and published under the title *The Road of Hope*.

Van Thuan was eventually released from prison in 1988, but was kept under house arrest until he was expelled from Vietnam in December 1991. Pope John Paul II welcomed him to Rome, where he was appointed President of the Pontifical Council for Justice and Peace, a post he held until his death in 2002.

'The hardest thing above all', Van Thuan later admitted,

was that I began to feel helpless. My plans, my activities, my efforts, were all for nothing. This practical helplessness described my condition for thirteen years. I wanted to do so many things to serve my people, but I could not.

He later realised that his plight and circumstances would lead to an altogether different ministry:

When the Communists put me in the hold of the boat, along with fifteen hundred other prisoners, and moved us to the north, I said to myself, 'Here is my cathedral, here are the people God has given me to care for, here is my mission – to ensure the presence of God among these, my despairing, miserable brothers. It is God's will that I am here. I accept his will.'

Writing about Van Thuan in his book *Dethroning Mammon*, Archbishop Justin Welby noted that, throughout his time in prison, Van Thuan managed to celebrate Communion and declare his joy in meeting God through the sacrament. Though he had no books, he celebrated by reciting the liturgy he had memorised over the years, and offering up to God, in the palm of his hand, a single grain of rice and a few drops of rice wine. Through long years of solitary confinement and torture, he was never released from his situation, but found himself embraced each day by the joy of God's love and grace. His refusal to give in to hopelessness and his determination to be sustained by a vision of hope had consequences for others around him. Van

Thuan led his torturers to Christ. He converted, taught and ordained priests in prison.

After his death, Pope Benedict XVI said of Van Thuan:

> During thirteen years in jail, in a situation of seemingly utter hopelessness, the fact that he could listen and speak to God became for him an increasing power of hope and joy, which enabled him, after his release, to become for people all over the world a witness to hope – to that great hope and joy which does not wane even in the nights of solitude.

However, as the season of Advent reminds us, it can be difficult to hold on to those signs and to trust in God's promises when we find ourselves in the midst of darkness.

The much-loved theologian Henri Nouwen mused on the difference between joy and happiness. While happiness is dependent on external conditions, joy, he wrote, is 'the experience of knowing that you are unconditionally loved and that nothing – sickness, failure, emotional distress, oppression, war, or even death – can take that love away'.[1]

Reflecting on his own experience, Nouwen continues:

> Joy is not the same as happiness. We can be unhappy about many things, but joy can still be there because it comes from the knowledge of God's love for us. I remember the most painful times of my life as times in which I became aware of a spiritual reality much larger than myself, a reality that allowed me to live the pain with hope … Joy does not simply happen to

us. We have to choose joy and keep choosing it every day.[2]

Questions for reflection

1 Where is joy to be found in your life ? Can you note the distinction between that joy and happiness, as described by Nouwen?

2 Van Thuan found immense strength and comfort in the sacrament of Holy Communion, which sustained him during his imprisonment. How does his experience inform your own understanding of the sacrament?

3 Van Thuan describes how his ministry was transformed after his arrest. Where is God calling you to minister? Who may he be asking you to care for?

Monday 18
Eglantyne Jebb

I do not travel well on tilting trains. There's something about the motion, the speed and the angle at which they're designed to go round corners that induces nausea in me akin to sea sickness. As a consequence, I am unable to carry out my usual travelling activities of writing, reading or working due to an inability to focus and the knowledge that, at some point, I'll end up face down on the table, battling with motion sickness, simply trying not to throw up.

Unfortunately, in December 2014 there was no alternative. The only travel option that evening on the London to Manchester route was on a tilting train and what should have been a celebratory journey, preparing to be part of a truly historic event the next morning – years in the making and months in the planning – was spent with a similarly afflicted colleague bemoaning our fate, as we counted the minutes to our destination. But we knew our journey would be worth it. For the following day, on which the extraordinary and tragically short life of the pioneer Eglantyne Jebb was commemorated in the church calendar, the Church of England was set to announce the appointment of its first woman bishop.

I confess I previously knew little of Eglantyne Jebb (1876–1928), a British social reformer and humanitarian. Born in Shropshire to a wealthy family, Eglantyne was educated at Lady Margaret Hall, Oxford. A short stint as a schoolteacher was followed by involvement in charity relief efforts, first in Cambridge and subsequently in Macedonia. In 1919, the impact of the Allied force's blockade upon children in Germany and Austria after the First World War led her to join the Fight the Famine Council and, with her sister Dorothy Buxton, to found the Save the Children fund. Eglantyne's initial aim was to provide food, clothing and medical care to children in need, but the organization quickly grew in size and scope and today it operates in more than a hundred countries, providing assistance to children affected by poverty, conflict and natural disasters.

In 1924, at the League of Nations convention in Geneva, Eglantyne presented a Declaration of the Rights of the Child she had written to leaders from around the world. This short but clear document asserted what she believed were the human rights of every child. The declaration was adopted in its original form a year later and in an extended one by the United Nations in 1959. Eglantyne died in 1928 at the age of 52, but her declaration later inspired the 1989 UN Convention on the Rights of the Child, a landmark human rights treaty. Jesus calls ordinary people to do extraordinary things in his name, whether those first disciples, tax collectors, fishermen and rebels who were enabled by the Holy Spirit to spread the good news far and wide, or those who, through their faith, have founded movements and organisations that have transformed the world.

A non-exhaustive list of such bodies, founded during the twentieth century alone by women and men following Christ, would include: the Samaritans, Oxfam, Help the Aged, Action Aid, Shelter, the Hospice Movement, Amnesty International, the Red Cross, Centrepoint and Save the Children.

The names of those who founded these organisations may be unfamiliar to us now – Chad Varah, Cecil Jackson Cole, Theodore Milford, Bruce Kenrick, Dame Cicely Saunders, Peter Benenson, Henry Dunant, Kenneth Leech and Eglantyne Jebb. Yet each of these, by placing their discipleship at the centre of their lives, helped to usher in the kingdom of God. The fruit of their work brought God's justice and love closer to people across our country and across the world, and their stories are worth telling and retelling.

Sadly, the dedication of these women and men has largely been airbrushed out of history, with barely any of the charities above making mention of the faith of their founders.

But to return to the opening of this reflection: on 17 December 2014, Downing Street announced that the Revd Libby Lane would be the next Bishop of Stockport. Minutes later, a press conference took place at Stockport Town Hall, and there Libby spoke of Eglantyne Jebb and her pioneering work:

On this historic day as the Church of England announces the first woman nominated to be Bishop, I am very conscious of all those who have gone before me, women and men, who for decades have looked forward to this moment. But most of all I am thankful to God.

Making history as a follower of Christ is not something many of us aim to do, let alone achieve. But sometimes we will live through times of historic change which serve as a reminder of the Spirit of God at work in our world, rejoicing in its fruit and being inspired in our faith.

It does not require the founding of a movement to change the world through faith. More often than not, lives can be transformed through the loving actions of individuals whose dedication to follow in the footsteps of Christ will be enough. Surely this is what Mother Teresa of Calcutta had in mind when she famously remarked: 'Do not attempt to do great things. Instead do small things with great love.'[3]

Yet whether through acts great or small, the invitation remains to change the world.

To go the extra mile, in your heart, for another, with great love.
To pray for our parishes and their people, with great love.
To pray for our Church and its future, with great love.
To pray expectantly for the Holy Spirit to lead the people of our villages, towns and cities so that this land would come to know Jesus Christ as Lord.
To do these small and great things with great love.
And through these things to change the world.
For as disciples our call is surely nothing less.

Questions for reflection

1 How aware are you of the Christian roots of many of our leading charitable organisations and movements for change? Did the list given surprise you?

2 What other organisations or movements can you think of which have been inspired by Christian movements?

3 Does it matter that the faith of the founders of these movements seems to have been airbrushed from history? Would a wider knowledge of their faith serve as an inspiration or division?

Tuesday 19

The Rt Revd Francis Loyo

There is much, perhaps too much, written about leadership these days. And occasionally, writing about our own leadership is demanded of us.

For many young people, there's the dreaded Personal Statement that accompanies an application to university, requiring them to tell of astonishing leadership while still in their teens. Elsewhere on these forms or in job applications, there's generally an encouragement to list your achievements – from exam or degree results right through to first aid, hygiene or road-safety cycling certificates – anything that confirms how great you are. But in my experience, the most inspiring leaders don't need to produce written records of achievement. Rather, it is simply through seeing and hearing about how they have led that they inspire and teach others.

Christian leadership was a required module in my training to be a priest. The course was useful in introducing different models of team dynamics, varying personality types and other tools. But the stand-out session came when one of the postgraduate students at the time, a bishop from Southern Sudan, agreed to give a reflection on his own ministry and leadership.

As Bishop Francis Loyo spoke about his experiences as the Bishop of Rokon, we found his humility breathtaking and his humour infectious. This was the first time he had been away from the diocese for a sustained period for many years. He was missing his wife Linda and the children they cared for, both his own and those whose parents had been killed in the decades-long civil war, in which more than 4 million people had been displaced and an estimated 2 million had died. During the war, Bishop Francis was imprisoned and his family fled into the bush. They thought one another dead for many years, before eventually being reunited by relief agencies.

As a bishop whose area covered both rebel-held territory and government-controlled land, his diocese formed part of the front line in the civil war. While many priests and bishops fled as a result of the conflict, Bishop Francis chose to remain with his flock.

This had led to numerous arrests, beatings and torture. Ministry in Sudan had been complex enough, but ministry in a civil war was bewildering. A long deep scar on one his legs was a permanent reminder to this brave man of being strung up upside down by the police, after he had refused permission to allow a witch-doctor to conduct a ceremony in an Anglican cemetery.

During our leadership session, Bishop Francis spoke about the dangers of pride. On one occasion as he was travelling to conduct a confirmation service, he was stopped at a rebel-held checkpoint, and asked where he was going.

'I am a bishop travelling through my diocese to conduct a service,' he said.

'I am sorry, Bishop, you cannot continue,' came the curt reply.

Bishop Francis was insistent. There were people waiting to be confirmed; they must let him pass.

The men on the checkpoint refused. Eventually one of the men directed his gun to the bishop's face and informed him that he could go no further.

'It was my wife, Linda, who saved my life that day,' he said. 'I was insistent that nobody would stop me going to church. I was a bishop and that was my purpose. She came up to me, took me to one side and told me that I would bring no honour to Christ, the church, my family or to anyone else if I got myself killed. I would have tried to keep going, but she talked sense to me.'

In January 2005, a few weeks after Bishop Francis gave that lecture, the Comprehensive Peace Agreement was signed in Sudan. Bishop Francis shed tears of joy as the news was announced. 'I have lived my whole life in war,' he said. 'The peace of Christ has come to Sudan.' He returned to the country later that year and continued his work, under some of the most difficult conditions imaginable, and created an orphanage, a school and a small hospital.

Writing in 1999 to mark the centenary of the Episcopal Church of Sudan, Bishop Francis noted that:

The driving force behind the Church in Sudan lies in the righteousness of faith which is founded on reconciliation through God. The Christian community in the Sudan begins at the very point where fences and walls are set up between human beings, where nations are divided, countries are separated, and families are split. The Church in the Sudan must resist every kind of separation if it wants to remain the community of the Church and to minister to people. It is only when congregations can be made up of Black and Arab, poor and rich, uneducated and educated, handicapped and non-handicapped, that there will be a witness to divine reconciliation in this hostile Sudan.[4]

After his return to Sudan, Bishop Francis twice stood to become Archbishop. In 2008, after coming second in the first round of elections, he withdrew his candidacy and urged his brother bishops to unite around Daniel Deng, who was duly elected as the fourth Primate and Archbishop of Sudan. Francis subsequently served as Dean of the Province of the Episcopal Church of South Sudan, in addition to continuing in his role as Bishop of Rokon. Ten years later, at the urging of others, he was nominated again to stand for Archbishop. As before, having fallen short in the first round of voting, he withdrew, urging others to unite around another candidate.

The Rt Revd Francis Loyo Mori died in October 2021 in hospital in Uganda and was subsequently buried in Rokon. His life of service, and the blessing that it brought to many, is echoed in the prayer of Ignatius of Loyola, and speaks more of leadership than a thousand texts.

Teach us, good Lord,
to serve you as you deserve,
to give and not to count the cost,
to fight and not to heed the wounds,
to toil and not to seek for rest,

to labour and not to ask for any reward,
save that of knowing that we do your will.[5]

Questions for reflection

1 What are the key ingredients of good leadership? Do these change at all in the context of church leadership?
2 Who do you think of as an example of a good leader? Why?
3 What does it mean in practical terms to be a servant leader? Does this change in the context of a conflict situation such as in Sudan and South Sudan?

Wednesday 20
Stormzy

The Lumiere festival in Durham, which is staged over four nights every other year, draws around two hundred thousand people into the city centre, where they come to marvel at the artistic light installations and displays. Situated in the centre of Durham, St Nic's opened its doors wide in 2019 and welcomed thousands into the church. The nave was transformed into a café space with live music, while the chapel area became an art exhibition with various images of Jesus on display, inviting people to enter into conversation about the Light of the World.

Each evening ended with the church playing an excerpt from the 2019 Glastonbury Festival. The headliner that year was the rap artist Stormzy, who appeared on the Pyramid stage alongside a gospel choir, introducing his final song by saying: 'Glasto, we're going to take this to church and we're going to give God all the glory right now. We're giving God all the glory.' He then launched into 'Blinded by Your Grace Part 2' with its refrain about brokenness and grace.

The performance is mesmerising for audience and performer alike because, not long into the song, Stormzy stops, takes in the sight of tens of thousands of people singing about God's grace, and falls to one knee in seeming disbelief at the sight before him. I never tire of watching

it. It is still available here: https://www.youtube.com/
watch?v=DxsjQ967kV8.

Afterwards, Stormzy explained that the reason for his
action was as much technical as spiritual.

> The sound absolutely blew and it was a total night-
> mare. I thought it was the worst thing I'd ever done
> and I thought I'd fumbled everything on the biggest
> stage of my career. At the time, my mum wasn't
> watching me at Glastonbury because her pastor had
> a vision that my performance was going to go wrong,
> so my mum was at church the whole time and she was
> praying for me and speaking in tongues. My mum's
> a prayer warrior. Even in my darkest times, God has
> been there.

His mother's faith and its impact upon his own belief is
something Stormzy often mentions, and has sung about in
a collaboration with J. P. Cooper on the track 'Momma's
Prayers'. That's a song I'd always wanted to play and show
in church on Mothering Sunday, but the animated film
accompanying it was adjudged to be a little too scary
for the younger members of the congregation. Another
reason for wanting to include it was that it's one of the few
Stormzy songs that talks about faith but doesn't contain a
huge amount of swearing – the strong language in others
makes sharing his music in a Christian context rather
problematic.

Stormzy acknowledged this contradiction when record-
ing his first album:

I needed to make an album that represented me, which was always going to be a struggle. I wanted to touch on the gospel side of things, and my faith, because that's so integral to my character. And the other side of my life – growing up in the streets, doing the things I've done with the people I was with, that is also a very integral part of me. I'm not a one-dimensional character.

Yet for many Christians, no matter how true to life or relevant the messages of the artist, no matter how authentic the music, the profanity is hard to get past.

Michael Ebenazer Kwadjo Omari Owuo Jr – to give Stormzy his real name – is an unlikely evangelist. In 2020, he received the Sandford St Martin Trustees' Award for his contribution to the public understanding of religion – not least in part due to his Glastonbury performance. The Chair of the Trust, Bishop Helen-Ann Hartley, highlighted that

the openness and clarity with which Stormzy speaks and sings about his faith and the efforts he's made to translate that into action resonates [sic] with people around the world who have heard his music on the radio, seen him perform on television or watched his videos online.

In accepting the award, Stormzy reflected on his faith journey and its public nature:

God's always been a very integral part of my life from when I was a kid and my mum used to take me to church. Then I started growing up and got to know him for myself. I've always said every award I've ever collected, every achievement I've ever had, I've always been vocal about the fact that it's not possible without God. God is the literal foundation. He's everything. He's the reason I'm here today. He's the reason I'm able to have a career ... a lot of the time I get non-believers saying, 'Don't thank God, this wasn't God. This was all you,' and I know this wasn't all me. This was God.

It was a theme Stormzy returned to two years later, when he was awarded an honorary degree by the University of Exeter for philanthropy and widening participation in education. Earlier that year, the *Sunday Times* placed him at number 11 on its annual Giving List, reflecting the millions of pounds that he'd donated to charitable causes, his funding of scholarships to the University of Cambridge, and his pledge to give away £10 million more to organisations, charities and movements involved in tackling racial inequality.

Receiving the degree in front of his mother, Stormzy said:

I strongly believe there is something that God has instilled in all of us and I thank him for giving me the courage to act upon it ... I've been so richly blessed by God and I don't just mean financially; I mean with love and life and family and joy, peace and purpose. To put it simply: I've beared [sic] fruit and shared fruit, and that's what we are all meant to do in whatever way we can … So to God be the glory and bless you all.

Questions for reflection

1 Stormzy has reflected that he struggles with being held up as a role model, acknowledging that his life is far from perfect. At the same time, he speaks openly about his Christian faith. Is it possible to deal with public figures who acknowledge their shortcomings without throwing stones?

2 Does the profanity in Stormzy's music mean that he shouldn't be viewed as a role model for other Christians? Is this akin to missionaries learning the language of the mission field to which they are called?

3 Who would you say are the best role models for young people today?

Thursday 21
Charlie Freer Andrews

The bringing down of the statue of Edward Colston in Bristol led to a nationwide debate. During his life, Colston was a renowned and respected philanthropist, giving away considerable amounts of his wealth to charitable causes, and the city of Bristol paid tribute to his work and generosity. But the source of Colston's wealth included the monies derived from his involvement with London's Royal African Company. During his 11-year association, it is estimated that around 80,000 slaves were embarked on to ships and around 20% of them died on the passage across the Atlantic.

Whether in civic spaces or in churches, the question about whom we memorialise and how has caused a great deal of soul-searching. Much of the focus has been on those already honoured, but it's worth considering too which other lives might we wish to celebrate and commemorate.

Among those would who make it to the top of my list is an often-overlooked English clergyman from the North-East of England. Nurtured in the West Midlands, he's already honoured in the calendar of saints in the Episcopal Church in the USA, and his face has appeared on stamps in India. Yet his life and work have largely been forgotten in England.

Charlie Freer Andrews was born in 1871 in Newcastle and was one of fourteen children. When he was still young, he moved to Birmingham with his family and completed his education at Pembroke College, Cambridge. He trained for the priesthood and spent time serving in churches and missions in Monkwearmouth and London, before being ordained a priest in the Church of England in 1897. After serving as Vice Principal of Westcott House in 1904, Andrews moved to India as a missionary with the Society for the Propagation of the Gospel. Here began a decade of teaching at St Stephen's College in Delhi, where he was to discover his lifelong vocation as a friend to the poor and an advocate for both India and the Indian diaspora.

It was actually in South Africa that Andrews first met the man for whose company and friendship he would be best remembered. At the time, 44-year-old lawyer Mohandas K. Gandhi was leading civil liberties campaigns against racially discriminatory pass laws. The long association and mutual impact the men had on each other's lives would later be reflected in Gandhi's comment, 'I have the honour to know hundreds of honest Christians, but I have not known one better than Andrews.'[6] He affectionately nicknamed Andrews Christ's First Apostle, based on his initials C. F. A.

It didn't take long for Andrews to promote the interest of Indians. Not long after his arrival as a tutor at St Stephens College, he declined the role of Principal in order to enable S. K. Rudra to become, in 1907, the first Indian principal of the college, and the first Indian to hold such a post in any Christian missionary or theological college.

Andrews went on to be a key supporter of the Free India movement, working with the fledgling Congress party and accompanying Gandhi to round table talks with the British Government. Yet despite his key role in the support of the movement for Indian independence, Andrews' greatest legacy and achievement were arguably in connection with the millions of Indians who became trapped in the British Government's 'Great Experiment' in the post-emancipation world of indentured labour.

After the abolition of slavery in the British Empire in the 1830s, a new system was established, initially at the request of plantation owners in the West Indies, to obtain 'a supply of Hill Coolies from Bengal' to be imported as indentured labourers for a period of five years.[7] Indentured labourers were hired by British colonies in the West Indies, Africa and South-East Asia to work on sugar, cotton and tea plantations, as well as rail-building projects. Indeed, between 1837 and the time the system ended in 1917, more than 1 million Indians served in 19 British colonies including Fiji, Mauritius, Ceylon, Trinidad, Guyana, Malaysia, Uganda, Kenya and South Africa.

Andrews visited many of these places in his work, bringing an end to the 'modern slavery' of bonded labour across the Empire, but it was his work in Fiji especially that led to the name that appeared on the stamp issued by the Indian Government in his honour in 1971: *Deenbandhu* – 'friend of the poor'. Two of his biographers highlight how, even after his battle to end indenture was won, he continued working in public health and education, seeking to provide welcome and housing to those labourers returning from Fiji and Guyana.

Charlie Andrews died in April 1940 at the age of 69 during a visit to India and is buried in the Lower Circular Road cemetery in Kolkata. Part of his life story was retold in Richard Attenborough's Oscar-winning film *Gandhi*, which emphasized the deep friendship of the men in South Africa and their work for Indian independence.

At the time of Andrews' death, seven years before independence, Mahatma Gandhi again paid tribute to his friend:

Not one of the heroic deeds of Andrews will be forgotten as long as England and India live. If we really love Andrews' memory we may not have hate in us for Englishmen, of whom Andrews was among the best and noblest.[8]

The Bengali polymath, Sir Rabindranath Tagore, with whom Andrews also developed a lifelong friendship, said a year after Andrews' death:

It has been my privilege to come in contact with big-hearted Englishmen of surpassing goodness, and it is on account of them that I have not lost faith in the people to whom they belonged. Andrews' memory perpetuates for me the nobility in the British heart. I have counted men like him as my own intimate friends and they are friends of all humanity. To have known such men was for me an enrichment of my life.[9]

There can be few clergymen who have had as bold an impact, not only upon the history of a nation but also upon its scattered peoples, than Charlie Andrews. His is a story of which we should be rightly proud. Whether in Newcastle where he was born, Birmingham where he was brought up or Cambridge where he taught, it would be a delight see a statue honouring his work and life. And it would be fitting too, if we followed the example of the Episcopal Church to remember him in our calendar of commemorations for the Church of England.

Questions for reflection

1 Whose life would you want to see celebrated with a statue or memorial?
2 How would you reflect on the relationship between indentured servitude and what we now refer to as 'modern slavery'?
3 Charlie Andrews could point to India and his ministry as his life's work. Where would your life's work for the gospel be found? What shape does it take?

Friday 22
The Revd Billy Graham

I was not born into a Christian household.

As I've mentioned, my mother is from a Hindu family and my father from a Sikh one. My dad died when I was a child and my respect for my mum, and my gratitude for all she sacrificed to raise my brother and me, knows no bounds. That gratitude includes accompanying me, one day in 1984, to the home ground of my beloved Aston Villa.

As someone born and brought up in Birmingham, it was only natural that I would support my local team. In the late 1970s and early eighties, I hadn't been allowed to go to Villa Park because the football grounds back then were rife with racism, and the National Front and British National Party ran a good trade in recruitment. My mum was probably right in thinking that Villa Park wasn't the best place for a chubby 13-year-old Asian boy to be.

But in 1984, walking home from school, I passed a poster outside my local church that said there was going to be an event at the ground. The church would be laying on coaches for all who wanted to go. And the coaches would be free.

I wasn't sure about the exact nature of the event. It was titled a 'Crusade', and the picture on the poster was of a man called Billy Graham. I had no idea who or what Billy Graham was, but I badgered my mum to let me go and eventually she agreed. At last, I had my chance to worship at the temple of Villa Park.

When I got there that night, Billy Graham talked about Jesus. He spoke about a living faith in a living God; about forgiveness, freedom and a new life in Christ. At the end of his message, he invited people to come down on to the hallowed turf to pray a prayer of commitment. I got up out of my seat, turned to my mum and asked her if I could go. When she said yes, I walked down and stood on the pitch, that holy ground, and invited Jesus into my life.

I got home buzzing, excited and joyful, and lay in bed, talking to God as if he were sitting in the chair right next to me. I have never forgotten that night, never forgotten how different, new and wonderful it felt. But for the following two years, I didn't go anywhere near a church. It wasn't that I didn't want to, rather it was that I didn't know how to. I didn't know any Christians, and I was wary of walking into an unfamiliar building with a pointy roof and making a fool of myself. It was only at the invitation of a friend a couple of years later that my church-going habit began (see 3 December).

According to the football club, a combined total of more than 257,000 people came to hear Billy Graham in Villa Park in the summer of 1984.

Fifty years earlier, as a 16 year old, Billy Graham had himself responded to the call of a travelling evangelist, giving his life to Christ at a revival meeting led by Mordecai Ham in Charlotte, North Carolina in 1934.

In the 55 years of itinerant ministry that followed, it is estimated that Billy Graham preached the gospel in person to more than 215 million people in more than 185 countries around the world. One report estimated that his lifetime audience, which included years of radio and television addresses and latterly internet broadcasts, was in excess of 2 billion.

'Until the twentieth century, the extent of an evangelist's outreach was determined by the limits of his voice and the distribution of his writings,' said Graham. 'Within the last few years, it has literally become possible to proclaim the gospel to the entire world. If Jesus were here today, I have no doubt he would make use of every means possible to declare his message.'

Twenty-eight years before Villa Park, in February 1956, Billy Graham went on his first crusade to India. In Kottayam in the south of the country, he spoke for three nights, drawing a crowd of 100,000 people each time. One of those who attended was Annamma Lukose.

Sally – as she was known to her family – came from a Christian family, her postmaster father being a member of the Orthodox Church and her mother an Anglican. But it was hearing Billy Graham speak about the saving work of Jesus Christ that led 16-year-old Sally to give her life to him that night.

Two years later, Sally told her parents that she wanted to become a nurse, a decision shaped by the nurturing and developing of her faith in the churches of Kerala. After studying in Mangalore, Mysore and Chandigarh, she settled in Bangalore where she took up a post as a nurse in a leprosy hospital.

Sally married a local farmer eight years after starting work, and brought up her three children in the nursing quarters provided by the hospital. Her youngest son would often accompany her on the seventy-minute bus journey to church each Sunday. He witnessed his mother's faith in action on a daily basis, not only in her loving care of her patients, but also in her routine of waking to listen to the Gospel Hour radio show at 5 a.m. each morning. He told me,

> She often used to weep when she prayed; she didn't know where else to turn. There was so much broken-ness in her working world she was desperate to find comfort which was provided in scripture, prayer and the person of Jesus Christ.

Sally's son followed his mother's faith and studied at theological college in India for three years before coming to the UK, where he eventually found himself training for ordained ministry in the Church of England. On 25 January 2022 – sixty-six years after Billy Graham preached in Kottayam – Sally's son, the Revd Malayil Lukose Varghese Muthalal, known as Saju, was consecrated as the Bishop of Loughborough in St Paul's Cathedral.

Questions for reflection

1 Billy Graham said that 'if Jesus were here today … he would make use of every means possible to declare his message'. Do you think the Church could do more to engage with digital media to declare the good news? How would it do this?

2 Watch some of Billy Graham's sermons online. What is it about his message that led so many people to respond to his invitation?

3 If someone were to ask you why they should become a
  Christian, or to share what you believed, what would
  you say? Do you dread the thought of someone asking
  you that question or would you welcome it?

Saturday 23

The Revd Dr Florence Li Tim-Oi

It was late as I sat at my desk in a deserted Church House in Westminster. I was online, reading news reports from around the world and trying to respond to the enquiries that were flooding in. My call list included the *Washington Post*, the *Sydney Morning Herald*, CNN, about a dozen BBC outlets, and broadcasters from Canada, Australia and the USA.

Hours earlier that day, on Wednesday 21 November 2012, the Church of England's General Synod had voted against the ordination of women as bishops. The proposal needed two-thirds majorities in each of the Synod's three houses to pass. The votes were 44 for and 3 against with 2 abstentions in the House of Bishops, 148 for and 45 against in the House of Clergy, and 132 for and 74 against in the House of Laity. The vote in the House of Laity, at 64%, was just 6 votes short of the required majority for the legislation to pass.

Television news was dominated by church members responding to the vote. More than one interviewee said that, for the first time in their lives, they were ashamed to be members of the Church of England. In rather unfortunate timing, a long-planned reception for members of the media, hosted by the Archbishop of Canterbury at Lambeth Palace, took place days later. One prominent television journalist and news anchor remarked how both of his daughters – neither of whom were church-going – had passionately reacted to the Synod's decision with great dismay, as it confirmed to them their worst fears about the Church.

Rowan Williams, the outgoing Archbishop of Canterbury, who had campaigned personally for a 'yes' vote, responded to the Synod's decision with sadness:

I would say first of all that I can well understand that feeling of rejection and unhappiness and deep perhaps disillusion with the institutional Church that many women may be feeling. I would also say it is still your Church and your voice matters and always will be heard and it is important therefore not to give up.

Half a world away and more than a century before that Synod vote, the first woman to be ordained as a priest in the Anglican Communion was born in the fishing village of Aberdeen on Hong Kong island. The Revd Dr Florence Li Tim-Oi arrived on 5 May 1907, one of eight children. With limited funds to educate her and her five brothers and two sisters, Li Tim-Oi did not complete her schooling until her early twenties. It was then that she heard the call to ministry at the ordination of an English deaconess in Hong Kong Cathedral. The Chinese preacher at the service asked if there were Chinese women also willing to be sent and serve the Chinese church. Li Tim-Oi later recollected that she knelt and prayed: 'God, would you like to send me?'

Ten years later, Florence Li Tim-Oi was ordained as a deacon by the Bishop of Hong Kong, Ronald Hall, on Ascension Day 1941. She was given charge of the Anglican congregation in the Portuguese colony of Macao, a neutral territory in the ongoing military conflict between China and Japan. The subsequent Japanese occupation of China meant that Anglican priests were unable to travel from Japanese-occupied territory to preside at the Eucharist. Responding both to the emergency in his diocese and the gifts he saw in his deacon, Bishop Hall ordained Florence Li Tim-Oi as a priest on 25 January 1944.

Her ordination was controversial, and due to the pressure of ecclesiastical concern, Florence resigned her licence after the end of the war in 1946, although she remained an ordained priest. In the years of the Maoist persecution that followed, she was unable to exercise her priesthood or even express her Christian faith openly. The Communist government in China closed all churches from 1958 to 1974, during which time Florence was compelled to work on a farm and to undergo political re-education. Three decades after her ordination, she resumed the practice of her priesthood in the Church in China, and then in Toronto where she joined her family and subsequently retired in 1981.

In January 1984, during a visit to England, the fortieth anniversary of her priesting was celebrated in her presence in Westminster Abbey. As part of the visit, she was invited to Lambeth Palace to meet Archbishop Robert Runcie, then unconvinced if women should be ordained to the priesthood. After meeting Florence he reportedly told the Canadian Archbishop Ted Scott: 'Who am I to say whom God can or cannot call?'

The Revd Dr Florence Li Tim-Oi died on 26 February 1992 in Toronto, where she was laid to rest. In November of that year, the General Synod of the Church of England voted to ordain women to the priesthood and in 1994, 50 years after Florence Li Tim-Oi's ordination, 1,500 women deacons were ordained. It would be another 20 years before the Synod finally voted to ordain women to the episcopate.

The Li Tim-Oi Foundation was set up by Florence's sister and Canon Christopher Hall, the son of Bishop Ronald Hall, in 1994. Li Tim-Oi's family had not been able to afford the cost of her course when she wanted to study for the ordained ministry, and others stepped in to pay. Today, the Foundation gives educational grants to women, both lay and ordained, who are members of an Anglican Church, or of a Church in communion with it. To date, more than 600 women from 124 dioceses in 14 provinces of the Anglican Communion, including Africa, Brazil, Fiji and India, have benefited. Those who receive the grants are known as 'the daughters of Li Tim-Oi'.

One of the first alumnae was the Revd Canon Dr Edidah Mujinya, an orphan whose guardians could not afford funding for her secondary education. In 1994, the Foundation paid for the three-year BD course that proved a springboard to fulfilling her potential. Edidah subsequently studied for a Masters and PhD from Makerere University, and is Vice Chancellor of Ankole West University and Provincial President of the Mothers' Union for the Church of Uganda.

Writing on behalf of ten Ugandan 'daughters of Li Tim-Oi' she reflected:

We are forever grateful for the support you ungrudg-ingly rendered to many of us, women you have not known, who are so far away and of varied cultures. When many of us had lost hope, were helpless, and stuck in a seemingly impossible situation, you came to our rescue. We are challenged. You have given us a sense of belonging, worthiness and a position in society – things that had almost disappeared. You have truly empowered us and we are committed as change agents to empower many others.[10]

Questions for reflection

1 It has been said of Li Tim-Oi that she suffered, not only at the hands of the Chinese Red Guard who made her cut up her vestments, but also at those of the Church's Purple Guard who pressured her to resign her post at the end of the war. Given the controversy of her ordina-tion, do you feel she was right to resign?

2 The General Synod eventually voted to enable women to be bishops in the Church of England by ensuring that both proponents and opponents of women's ordination to the episcopate could 'mutually flourish'. Does such compromise reflect a central strength or weakness of the Anglican approach?

3 The life and ministry of Florence Li Tim-Oi speaks of trial, waiting and hope. How might we sustain others who find themselves in such stages of life?

Christmas Eve

The Revd Dr Martin Luther King:
stick with love

Not long after the murder of George Floyd in May 2020, I sat down with a friend in the Bishop's Mill, the local Wetherspoon's pub in Durham city centre. Despite the owners' politics being somewhat at variance to my own (and the rather sticky carpet underfoot), the free Wi-Fi and cheap coffee (with no-cost refills) made it my de facto meeting place.

My friend and I spoke about the Church, racism and Black Lives Matter. In an unguarded moment, she asked how I was feeling, and I found myself pouring out about how the murder of George Floyd had brought back much of what I had managed to box away and leave well alone. I spoke about the years I'd spent being involved in racial justice campaigns. I remembered the demonstrations I'd been on over the decades for the young men whose lives had ended with racist violence – Ricky Reel, Rohit Duggal, Rolan Adams and Stephen Lawrence. I talked about the time I sat in a meeting in Birmingham's Council House to organise a conference on anti-racism, only for the meeting to be overrun by thugs who turned up to abuse us. The fear I felt as the police escorted me home through the city centre that night is still a vivid memory. I recalled being approached at Birmingham New Street station and told by a stranger that I should watch myself, and that my name was on the Combat 18 hitlist (Combat 18 was a violently fascist paramilitary organisation operating in the UK in the 1990s, the numbers 1 and 8 referring to the initials of Adolf Hitler's name). My friend and I talked about the times I had experienced racism in the Church that I loved, and about how our vocation to be a Church of all nations, colours, races and tribes – not only across nations but in nations – seemed to be failing desperately. In short, I had had enough. I had given up on the Church and race. I had played my part and now it was for others. Sitting at a table in that Wetherspoon's, I began to weep. It wasn't a good look.

But in the months that followed, I found myself working as part of the Archbishops' Anti-Racism taskforce to produce a report we entitled *From Lament to Action*. Despite the internal opposition to the report from some quarters (including the leaking of a draft to a publication guaranteed to oppose it), it led to some positive action, although not all that we had asked for and not all that had been promised.

Years earlier, as I was looking for a biography of Martin Luther King, I came across a book by David Garrow entitled *Bearing the Cross*. It is not a hagiography, and through it, I discovered things about Dr Martin Luther King that I never previously knew. I learned of his vanity for fine clothes. I learned of the adulterous affairs which he conducted while he was married and his wife was at home looking after their small children. I learned that this man – a hero of mine since my teenage Christian years – had feet of clay and was, like me, a sinner.

Yet I also came to know how God used him. A key moment in the book focused on one January evening in 1956, when Dr King was at home and had received a threatening phone call. It included yet another death threat to him and his family. Dispirited, depressed and unable to sleep, he sat at his kitchen table wrestling with his own dark night of the soul. He began to pray:

Lord, I'm down here trying to do what's right. I am here taking a stand for what I believe is right. But Lord, I must confess that I'm weak now, I'm faltering. I'm losing my courage. Now, I am afraid. And I can't let the people see me like this because if they see me weak and losing my courage, they will begin to get weak. The people are looking to me for leadership, and if I stand before them without strength and courage, they too will falter. I am at the end of my powers. I have nothing left. I've come to the point where I can't face it alone.[11]

As he prayed alone in the silent kitchen, King heard a voice saying, 'Martin Luther, stand up for righteousness. Stand up for justice. Stand up for truth. And lo, I will be with you. Even until the end of the world.' King later disclosed: 'I heard the voice of Jesus saying still to fight on. He promised never to leave me, never to leave me alone. No never alone.'[12]

Fourteen years later, in August 1967, Dr King addressed the Southern Christian Leadership Conference on the topic 'Where Do We Go from Here?'

As part of his address, he spoke of the need to refrain from responding to hatred with hatred. Rather, he argued, it was absolutely necessary to stick with love:

I'm concerned about a better world. I'm concerned about justice; I'm concerned about brotherhood; I'm concerned about truth ... And I say to you, I have also decided to stick with love, for I know that love is ultimately the only answer to mankind's problems. And I'm going to talk about it everywhere I go. I know it isn't popular to talk about it in some circles today. And I'm not talking about emotional bosh when I talk about love; I'm talking about a strong, demanding love. For I have seen too much hate ... and I say to myself that hate is too great a burden to bear. I have decided to love.

Just over six months later, on 3 April 1968, the day before he was assassinated, Martin Luther King spoke at a rally for striking workers in a church in Memphis. He wasn't worried about what life had in store, he said. He had been shot at, stabbed, vilified by the national media, and held up as a figure of hatred for his opposition to war in Vietnam. But he refused to be bowed, he refused to fear.

Martin Luther King ended his speech that night with a reference to Moses standing at the top of Mount Nebo, at the end of Israel's journey through the wilderness, surveying a land he would never enter but which represented God's promise to his people. Martin Luther King said:

Well, I don't know what will happen now. We've got some difficult days ahead. But it doesn't matter with me now. Because I've been to the mountain-top. And I don't mind. Like anybody, I would like to live a long life. Longevity has its place. But I'm not concerned about that now. I just want to do God's will. And he's allowed me to go up to the mountain. And I've looked over. And I've seen the promised land. I may not get there with you. But I want you to know tonight, that we, as a people, will get to the promised land. And I'm happy, tonight. I'm not worried about anything. I'm not fearing any man [sic]. Mine eyes have seen the glory of the coming of the Lord.

Questions for reflection

1 How it is possible to stick with love in the face of concerted hatred? How as agents of reconciliation can Christians both model and encourage this?

2 Advent can be a time for putting our spiritual affairs in order, including the reaffirmation of love over hate. Are there areas in our lives where we can detect hate that needs addressing?

3 Martin Luther King moved from being afraid at his kitchen table to not fearing any person. Where is such depth of courage to be found?

Notes

The first week of Advent

1 'Church history: Declaration of Independence', Hermon Marthoma Church, the Midlands, UK, https://www.midlandsmtc.org.uk/church-history/, accessed May 2023.

2 'Myriam's story and song', Sat-7 UK, YouTube, https://www.youtube.com/watch?v=_ige6CcXuMg, accessed May 2023.

3 H. Berhane, *Song of the Nightingale* (Milton Keynes: Authentic Media, 2009).

The second week of Advent

1 D. Adesina, '2018 Person of the Year: A goddess of resistance', *Guardian Nigeria*, 1 January 2019, https://guardian.ng/features/2018-person-of-the-year-a-goddess-of-resistance/, accessed May 2023.

2 P. Wilkinson, 'Retired priest speaks of bus-stop evangelism', *Church Times*, 14 February 2020.

3 Prayers at the Preparation of the Table, 1, *Common Worship*. Extracts from *Common Worship: Services and prayers* are copyright © The Archbishops' Council, 2000, and are reproduced by permission. All rights reserved, copyright@churchofengland.org.

4 'The Lucia tradition: What does midwinter have to do with white gowns and candles? It's Swedish Lucia!', 7 December 2022, https://sweden.se/culture/celebrations/the-lucia-tradition, accessed May 2023.

5 W. Wink, *The Powers That Be: Theology for a new millennium* (New York: Bantam Doubleday Dell, 2000).

6 W. Brueggemann, *The Bible Makes Sense* (London: Darton, Longman and Todd, 2016), p. 69.

7 John of the Cross, *The Dark Night of the Soul by St. John of the Cross*, trans. by David Lewis (London: Thomas Baker, 1908).

8 Mother Teresa, *Come Be My Light: The revealing private writings of the Nobel Peace Prize winner*, ed. by B. Kolodiejchuk (London: Rider, 2008).

9 D. Bonhoeffer, *God Is in the Manger: Reflections on Advent and Christmas* (Louisville, KY: Westminster John Knox Press, 2010).

10 A. Arora, 'Own goal by politicians who support the free speech of booing fans', *Northern Echo*, 8 December 2020, https://www.thenorthernecho.co.uk/news/18929847.goal-politicians-support-free-speech-booing-fans/, accessed May 2023.

11 D. Bonhoeffer, *Letters and Papers from Prison*, ed. by J. Bowden and S. Wells (London: SCM Press, 2017).

The third week of Advent

1 H. J. M. Nouwen, *Here and Now: Living in the Spirit* (London: Darton, Longman and Todd, 1994).

2 Nouwen, *Here and Now*.

3 Mother Teresa, *A Life for God: Mother Teresa treasury* (Grand Rapids, MI: Zondervan, 1996).

4 *But God Is Not Defeated! Celebrating the centenary of the Episcopal Church of Sudan, 1899–1999* (Nairobi: Paulines, 1999), pp. 39–40.

5 Prayer during the Day, *Common Worship: Daily Prayer*. *Common Worship: Daily Prayer* is copyright © The Archbishops' Council, 2005, and extracts are reproduced by permission. All rights reserved, copyright@churchofengland.org.

6 H. Tinker, *The Ordeal of Love: C. F. Andrews and India* (New Delhi: Oxford University Press India, 1998).

7 M. Mahoney, 'A "new system of slavery"? The British West Indies and the origins of Indian indenture', *The National Archives* blog, 3 December 2020, https://blog.nationalarchives.gov.uk/a-new-system-of-slavery-the-british-west-indies-and-the-origins-of-indian-indenture, accessed May 2023.

8 As quoted by Ramachandra Guha, 'Searching for Charlie: *The Telegraph*', Ramachandra Guha, 28 February 2009, https://ramachandraguha.in/archives/searching-for-charlie-the-telegraph.html, accessed May 2023.

9 R. Tagore, *Crisis in Civilisation and Other Essays* (New Delhi: Rupa Publications, 2003).

10 Li Tim-Oi Foundation, 'It takes ONE woman', https://www.ltof.org.uk/wp-content/uploads/pdfs/litimoi_booklet.pdf, accessed May 2023.

11 D. Garrow, *Bearing the Cross: Martin Luther King, Jr., and the Southern Christian Leadership Conference* (New York: William Morrow, 1986).

12 Garrow, *Bearing the Cross*.

The Big Church Read

Did you know that you can read

Stick with Love

as a Big Church Read?

Join together with friends, your small group
or your whole church, or do it on your own,
as Arun Arora leads you through the book.

Visit **www.thebigchurchread.co.uk** or use the **QR code below
to watch exclusive videos from Arun Arora**
as he explores the ideas and themes of *Stick with Love*.

**The Big Church Read will also provide you with a reading plan
and discussion questions** to help guide you through the book.

It's free to join in and a great way to read through
Stick with Love!